Praise for Marilyn McEntyre's Previous work

"Brings lively attention to the way words can open multiple doors of memory, imagination, and reflection."

—**Richard Rohr,** author of *Falling Upward*

"Marilyn McEntyre reminds us of the power of language—to heal and instruct us, to challenge and shape us."

—**Shauna Niequist,** author of *Present over Perfect*

"Encourages, guides, and directs. . . . Marilyn McEntyre embodies simple, patient kindness in her writing."

—**Michael Card,** singer/songwriter, author of *The Nazarene*

"McEntyre has again written with conspicuous grace and truth. . . . Some passages here are as powerful and lovely as any I've encountered in years."

—**Cornelius Plantinga,** author of *Gratitude*

"Seamlessly blending exegesis, philology, lectio divina, and prayer, Marilyn McEntyre teaches us how to listen for the divine word in all times and circumstances."

—**Carol Zaleski,** coauthor of *Prayer: A History*

"With her profound summonings, Marilyn McEntyre recovers for many contemporary readers an ancient practice that is reminiscent of rabbinic attention to the dark sayings of Scripture, those compelling, curious, often-challenging passages that would nudge us into seeing more, would have us glimpse the inexhaustibility of the One in Whom we live and move and have our being, even the inexhaustibility of His Word."

—**Scott Cairns,** author of *Idiot Psalms*

START with a WORD

On the Craft and Adventure of Writing

Marilyn McEntyre

William B. Eerdmans Publishing Company
Grand Rapids, Michigan

Wm. B. Eerdmans Publishing Co.
2006 44th Street SE, Grand Rapids, MI 49508
www.eerdmans.com

Published 2026
Printed in the United States of America

32 31 30 29 28 27 26   1 2 3 4 5 6 7

ISBN 978-0-8028-8316-2

Library of Congress Cataloging-in-Publication Data

A catalog record for this book is available from the Library of Congress.

CONTENTS

READ LIKE A WRITER

There is, then, creative reading as well as creative writing.

—Ralph Waldo Emerson

The first thing I remember reading, following my grandmother's finger as it moved across the page, was *Winnie the Pooh*. The first thing I remember writing sounded suspiciously like A. A. Milne, albeit whittled to child-sized sentences. Hearing stories in the familiar voices and cadences of beloved adults gave me a sense of what it meant to read: to bring life and breath to what lay on a page, to allow printed words to awaken feelings as real as any others—laughter at Pooh's befuddlements; tears at Beth March's quiet dying in *Little Women*; curiosity about where a clue might turn up for Nancy Drew. Reading to myself in my tree house on Saturday afternoons or hiding under the covers after bedtime with a flashlight equipped me for a writing life. Writing seemed a natural, sometimes necessary, response to anything worth reading. And reading taught me how to write—that and more than a few generous, underpaid teachers. Good writers still teach me how to write.

I learned to love sentences not just for what they said but for how they worked. I learned to love literary surprises—sudden turns of plot or phrase, shifts of perspective and mood, metaphors that reframed ordinary things and lines in poems that took my breath away. I read Psalms and stories from the King James Bible, memorized verses in Sunday school, and heard those antique words quoted in sermons. I read *To Kill a Mockingbird* tucked in a big chair while I recovered from tonsillitis. I don't remember the sore throat, but I do remember Atticus in the courtroom and Scout's visit to Calpurnia's church. I read Shakespeare and wanted to be as witty and free as Rosalind, as subversive as Viola, and as generous and forgiving as Cordelia. I read *Pride and Prejudice* and longed to speak like (if I couldn't actually be) Elizabeth Bennett. I read *Pilgrim at Tinker Creek* and learned from Annie Dillard how sudden shifts of frame and focus can lead you to what Abraham Heschel called "radical amazement." I don't speak like Elizabeth or write like Annie, but I do speak and write and continue to be surprised by what words can do.

For years I've taught and coached readers and writers, and what I have to say to readers is, if you want to read well, try writing now and then. Imitate someone's style. Write an open letter. Write a poem. Get on the other end of the pen. And to writers I say, if you want to write, read. Read slowly. Read curiously. And critically, and deeply, and imaginatively. Pause over sentences that wake you up and consider why. When Emerson reminded his readers, "There is, then, creative reading as well as creative writing," he was certainly aware of how many centuries of creative reading testified to that simple truth. The Jewish tradition of midrash, for example, is a rabbinical practice of broad, imaginative reading and interpretation designed, as Hebrew scholar Wilda Gafney put it, to "discern value in texts, words, and letters, as potential revelatory spaces."

What a wonderful way to think about reading: as a discernment process, a process of seeking and expecting revelation. Thoreau may have had a similar notion in mind when he wrote of his own life as a writer, "There are more secrets in my trade than most men's." Words reveal and conceal. There's something hovering unspoken, waiting to be discovered, behind every sentence. Every word choice casts its little bit of light into the darkness of unknowing. Leonard Cohen put it rather more memorably: "There is a blaze of light in every word." Well-chosen words invite and beckon and sometimes shock us into awareness. When we hear one, something changes—a habit of mind, a judgment—and something familiar is made strangely new.

Good readers go into a text equipped with questions. The first ones are simple: *What's going to happen? Where is this writer taking me? Do I trust them? Where are the surprises?* Then perhaps more reflective questions: *What is this writer inviting me to do? What am I hoping for? How do I decide whether to go on? Is this book worth fifteen hours of my life? What does it require of me?* If it doesn't require much of anything besides turning pages to see what happens next, it may be rather thin fare. And, importantly, *What do I have to let go of to get the gift that's being offered?*

I've raised that last question many times in response to students who found themselves put off by a writer's long digressions or cryptic allusiveness, or, more disturbingly, by language that betrayed unexamined attitudes common to an earlier generation, perhaps, but to some degree inappropriate or even offensive now. Those occasions arise not infrequently in American literature where a painful history of patriarchy, white privilege, racism, misogyny, and imperialism comes up either explicitly or implicitly in nearly every story we read, sometimes, though certainly not always, uncritically.

Good reading involves a social contract: we consent, at least provisionally, to the writer's terms, even if they're unconventional or odd. We agree to release ourselves from preconceptions; trying not to impose our notions about how history or detective fiction or a coming-of-age novel "should" be told. We postpone judgment, giving the writer a chance to make their case or complicate their characters. Good reading is open and generous, but not uncritical; able to appreciate ambiguity and paradox; able to contextualize; and to be compassionate. Compassion might not seem like a particularly "readerly" virtue, but it applies: reading is relational. A story or poem or play is an invitation by a fellow human being to reflect on how things happen; why they happen to some people and not others; how people acquire, use, and abuse power; how people cope with suffering, give one another occasion and permission to laugh, and learn to love and forgive, even in the worst of times.

As in friendship, there's often something to forgive, or at least background, as you look for what is of value. A male writer of a few generations back may give women short shrift. A white writer may narrate from a point of view that is somewhat blind to the privilege that point of view represents. But before you give up on a writer, do take a few moments to assess what might make the book worth reading. One critic called *Gravity's Rainbow* a "great steaming slag-heap of a novel," but he finished it and bothered to write about it. Sometimes there's treasure to be found under a slag heap.

Some barriers are too high. Some writers are superbly skillful and still give offense or do outright harm. When they do, we're free to close the book or change the screen. Every page we turn is a choice.

Each genre teaches us something unique and indispensable about how to read. Poetry, for example, imposes its own requirements. Poems demand that we slow down, notice patterns, reckon with ambiguities, consider subtle distinctions between one term or image and its alternative, and recognize the relationship between techniques and purposes. But if we take this work on, if we practice finding paths through poems, staying with them as we tease out their possibilities, follow where they point us by allusion and suggestion, and unpack their metaphors, they can equip us to walk into any situation, look around, assess, analyze, and act. They teach us to listen more attentively to language and to reckon more astutely with the arts of persuasion. More than that, they restore to us what I believe the noise and haste of commercial culture dull and destroy: attunement to subtleties of sense and feeling, awakeness to the possibilities of "an ordinary moment on an ordinary day." They train and exercise the imagination.

When you read poetry or prose, ask *how*, not *what*. Don't ask the big questions—ask the small questions. They're the big questions in disguise. *Why did he pick this word? Why did she choose to end the line here? What happens when the regular rhythm is broken in the third line? What shifts the tone in the final couplet?* Stop over anything that gives you pause. Take a word or an image, turn it over, examine it, and consider how it's behaving. If you march through the poem, left to right, top to bottom, you'll be at the end of it very quickly, having navigated the road but missed the landscape. Poems trick you that way. You have to learn to read all over again or you'll miss them altogether; they'll be over in sixty seconds, and you'll wonder where you've been.

When you allow yourself to be stopped suddenly, you may find your memories realigned by a surprising verb or image. Or maybe you find your curiosity piqued by a phrase that reframes something familiar in a way you've never considered. Pausing to make room for a felt response, you make yourself vulnerable to the action of the poem. You come into a curious intimacy shared by those who seek a healing word or a line that can bridge deep differences or lift us out of brokenness into a place of knowing. A good poem will model and require a quality of attention that can transform and sharpen our vision. It can make us more capable of gratitude and awe.

* * *

The *Tao Te Ching* teaches, "When the student is ready the teacher will appear." I've found that to be true in my reading and writing life. Haven't you had the experience of someone putting just the right book in your hand at the right time? Suddenly that writer becomes your teacher: the way they think, the way they move through a paragraph, their restraint or elegance or wild, sidelong leaps of association take you to a learning edge. Or they offer you a view from a very different culture or generation and a chance to explore the roots not only of your ideas and attitudes but of the words you rely on. You become linguistically self-aware.

Reading and writing well keep alive in us the desire to be precise, lively, surprising, hospitable, challenging, wise. They make us want to be good if only in the sense that choosing exact and appropriate words is a matter of choosing the good. There are certainly excellent writers who are not people of exemplary virtue, but I don't think you can be an excellent writer without developing *some* virtues, if only fidelity to a practice that honors the gift of language.

In the chapters that follow we'll be reflecting on the craft of writing, learning writing practices from practiced writers and how writing changes both writer and reader. I'll be inviting you to read like an apprentice—paying close attention to the moves good writers make and trying them out for yourself. Imitation opens a pathway to originality. If you imitate Keith Jarrett's piano improvisations, you may find yourself free and versatile enough to play the piano unlike him or anyone else. If you try now and then a sentence as deep and sustained as one of William Faulkner's or as bold and poignant as one of Toni Morrison's, you may find yourself making moves that take you and your readers to new depths.

Each of the coming chapters focuses on particular moves, practices, or skills. If this were a book about tennis, there would be chapters on the forehand, the backhand, footwork, net play, serving, and strategy. Similarly, we'll look at ways to begin, develop, digress, frame scenes, present characters, and conclude. We'll also look at ways to engage readers' imaginations, open their hearts, foster compassion, sharpen their sense of irony, and maybe help them embrace the ambiguities that remind us, as the poet Mark Van Doren put it, "There is no single way it can be told."

* * *

Before we move on, here are a few basic practices that can help sharpen your noticing skills and make you a more receptive, discerning, engaged reader. Obviously, you can't read in slow motion all the time, but if you read slowly and attentively now and then, it will make the rest of your reading life richer and more enjoyable:

1. Take a few minutes before reading to close your eyes, breathe slowly, focus on your breath, and let your mind clear itself.
2. Read a sentence at a time. Stop after every few sentences and let yourself repeat whatever word or image moves into the foreground.
3. Let associations emerge. Ask yourself: *Why did that word or image stop me? What does it bring to mind?*
4. Read as if the words were instructions. Ask yourself: *How does this text instruct me?*
5. Read as if the words were invitations. Ask yourself: *How does this text invite me?*
6. Read as if the words were poetry/song. Put part of the text, if it is prose, into poetic lines. If it is poetry, make up a melody for a few lines.
7. Read as if the words were a privileged secret. Ask yourself: *What is being disclosed that needs to be protected from misconstruction, misunderstanding, misuse?*
8. Consider and name the feelings the words evoke. Ask yourself: *Which words awaken those feelings?*
9. Be aware of your consent. Say "yes" periodically as you read—to whatever you can say yes to. Where a "yes" doesn't happen, say "no" or "maybe."
10. Pose deliberate questions as you read. Ask a question every few lines—just a simple question: *Why? How? What then? In what sense? What else? Meaning what?*

Let the writers you love teach you to write.

BEGIN BEGINNING

The end is where we start from.

—T. S. Eliot

Unless you're writing the book of Genesis, you can't begin at the beginning. There's always a backstory. You could start your memoir with your birth. Or your Lebanese grandmother's. Or the first time you played a clarinet solo. Or you could start it with what you saw out the window this morning as you were having your first cup of coffee. You could start a book on climate change with a simple explanation of how a combustion engine works, or with a paragraph about lizards who live in hot Saharan sand. So, with the understanding that you really can begin anywhere, let's consider, one by one, some of the many ways to make a beginning happen.

This chapter isn't about what you do after you find a way to begin. We'll get to that. Right now, take some time with beginning itself—to play with possibilities—beginning and beginning again until you find a few sentences or an opening line that gives you energy. I'll offer a variety of opening gambits—invitations to play around with beginnings as part of your practice.

Beginning is such an important part of writing anything, you can afford to spend time trying out different ways to do it. Each way will give you information. That information will likely come in the form of energy, or of an intuitive "click": all of us know the moment when we look at something we've written or chosen and say, "No, that's not quite it." And then the surge of pleasure that comes when we look at something else we've written and say, "That's it! That works. That nails it." It's the conviction many of us have when we're shopping for the right outfit for an occasion: I'm not sure what I'm looking for, but I'll know it when I see it. That trustworthy feeling of recognition is what to watch for as you try out ways to begin.

Writing is a mostly receptive process, at least for me. When I sit down to write, I don't always know where to begin. So, I listen to what comes up and say yes—okay—I'll start there and see what happens. If a phrase or sentence or line comes, I write it down, look at it and say thank you. But I don't always move on with it. Sometimes I scroll down to a new blank page and wait and listen some more for an alternative beginning. I do this several times—begin and then see where I am. I may end up with the first beginning I tried, but by the third or fourth start (I don't call them false starts—they're valuable experiments) I almost always have a sense of why one beginning works better than another.

* * *

Let's experiment. You may have a big idea but don't begin with it. Try beginning with one of these:

Begin with a word. Almost any word will do: *ticklish* . . . *rocking* . . . *gracious* . . . *custard* . . . *dolphins*. Whatever the word brings up will point a direction, so go there. You might try beginning with different kinds of words—verbs, nouns, prepositions, adverbs—just as a way of noticing what difference it makes which part of speech serves to open the door of narrative: like different keys with different shapes, they'll open different doors.

Opening sentences that start with pronouns are pretty common: *I, he, they* . . . did something you'll want to hear about.

An opening sentence that starts with a noun may offer an object of focus that is neither narrator nor character, but something we assume will matter: *Dishes lay unattended in the sink. Trees, charred and fallen, covered the hillside.*

A verb that's become a gerund or modifier opens with a different kind of energy than a noun: *Running the same course every morning, she began her days thinking only of weather and wind.*

The word you start with gives you a thread to tug on. Tug gently and see what thoughts and words follow: *Late afternoons we often saw dolphins at play not far from shore.* Or *Custard tastes a little better when you call it crème brulée.* There's more to say about dolphins. And custard. Listen and hear what comes next.

Start a sentence with one of these one-word prompts and see where it leads. It might lead you back to something you've been writing or wanting to write. It might start you on a poem or an essay or a letter to an editor.

Inexplicably . . .
Turning . . .
Ringtones . . .
Simply . . .
Mystery . . .
Pink . . .

Starting a sentence by simply writing a word down doesn't allow you to overthink before you begin. If you have no plan, the word will do its work unhindered, burrowing into memory or imagination and planting the seed of an idea. Just write it down. Then notice. If it's a modifier, it needs something to modify. If it's a noun, it's likely to want to be the subject. You can give yourself this kind of prompt every day—just let a word come and see where it wants to go.

• • •

Begin with an image. Notice what words come when you imagine, say, a music stand or a bowl of strawberries or the noonday sun that Yeats described as "blank and pitiless." See the image in your mind's eye: *an unlaced shoe . . . a withered bouquet . . . a map on the wall.* Say one thing about it. Then another. Describe it as closely as you can. Or say what it reminds you of. Or name the feeling it evokes and consider why.

When you start with an image, you lead with feeling. So, for example, if the point you want ultimately to make is "We desperately need gun control," you might begin your reflection with what a survivor saw after the shooting: scattered crayons or a chair on its side or a single shoe. When we imagine those abandoned objects, we know something is out of order and we are troubled, and we keep reading. The large issues that need to be thought about—background checks, protection of children, restriction of automatic weapons—can begin to emerge in ensuing paragraphs, but even as we move into legislative process or ballistics, we can't forget those crayons or that little shoe.

Dream images can be a rich source to draw on. Even if you don't record your dreams as narratives, you might try keeping a record of dream images for a period of time just to see what they evoke, how they keep coming up, how they may become invitations: a snake on the path, say, or a heavy door slightly ajar, or a cresting wave. Every image is an invitation.

* * *

Begin with a phrase. Prepositional phrases are fun to begin with; they always put you somewhere: *Around the corner . . . After the windstorm . . . Under the rubble . . .* As soon as you write down a prepositional phrase, you have some sense of time or place or situation: *On the top shelf I spied a dog-eared copy of "Middlemarch"* . . . gives us a sense of character, environment, and a past in which other readers preceded the one who speaks. Just finishing the sentence the phrase started gives you a plot point, and maybe a character: *After the windstorm they toured the outbuildings to assess the damage.* So much is already implied in that sentence. You have a couple of characters. They have a problem. They're probably lamenting bits of loss, considering repair work to be done and the expense of doing it. They're going to have decisions to make. And *you* now have decisions to make: Who are they? Spouses? Father and son? What tensions may arise as they look over damaged property? Have they done this before?

Prepositional-phrase prompts lead you to where something is bound to happen. Once you're there, you'll find out what you came for. Try completing sentences that start with one of these. See if a couple more sentences want to come, too. Or a whole paragraph. You might end up with a story.

Across the water
Among the trees
Just below the surface
Well into the following months
Beyond the imposing doors
On the hard pew

Of course, the phrase you begin with doesn't have to be a prepositional phrase. You could simply begin with a phrase you like for its color, its suggestiveness, its sound, the images it evokes: *the great silence . . . a handful of dust . . . carefully saying nothing.* If you find a phrase you like, sit with it and notice what it evokes. Hold the phrase and let a sentence grow around it. Let memories come up, colors, facial expressions, a landscape. A phrase like *the great silence*, for instance, might lead to a sentence about being on retreat in a monastery or camping in the woods. Or a reflection on how, in silence, you hear the voices within you, or, in deep silence, the voice of God.

Familiar-phrase prompts give you a backdrop—phrases you can't use without remembering *Hamlet* or the Gettysburg Address or the Sermon on the Mount. To use them is to let your reader hear the echo as well, though you may put them to your own very new purposes. Try putting any of these (or a familiar phrase from your own reading life) into the context of a few sentences. See how it adds resonance.

the bell tolls
flights of angels
these honored dead
the lilies of the field
through a glass darkly
in that number
less traveled by
to the mountaintop
a hard rain
a thousand points of light
never again
let it be

* * *

Begin with a sentence. Think about the famous opening sentences you know: *Call me Ishmael* or *I am an invisible man*. Or the much longer ones like the one that begins Faulkner's *Absalom, Absalom!* that covers most of a page. I won't quote it here, but look it up and consider all you've navigated and all you've inferred by the time you get to the end of it.

The opening sentence itself doesn't have to be syntactically impressive. A simple observation will do, for example: *Our neighbor's trees are dying*. Maybe yours aren't. Maybe you worry about what else is dying. Maybe you remember when a friend, swinging from a dead branch on a dying tree, fell and how he has never walked properly since. And how another friend lives with chronic guilt because he dared him to do it. And that makes you think about the complexities of moral responsibility—so you go there. Or maybe you've heard of Dutch elm disease, and you look it up and begin to write a reflective piece about how the nonhuman world suffers, too.

Here are a few sample observations to try out as starter sentences. Add a couple of sentences to one of them and see where they take you. You might end up with a poem. Or a research piece on sleep patterns. Or a reflection on how differently we navigate hard things. Or a short story peopled by characters you didn't know you knew, but they begin to emerge as you put more sentences down and pretty soon a whole constellation of relationships emerges as you connect the dots. You just have to begin by putting down some dots. Try any or all of these:

She woke before the sun rose.
They set their packs down.
He paused before opening the door.
Congress is back in session.
The wi-fi signal is weak.

Notice that most simple observations give you a sense of time, place, and situation. You're not just "anywhere." You're never just anywhere. Human situations and even the most abstract human thoughts happen somewhere, sometime, to someone. Even an essay on a topic as abstruse as "Calculus Made Simple" or "Teleological Reflections" is likely to provoke a reader's interest if it begins by pointing at something ordinary and real—something a person might have a feeling about—and offering an observation: *Math wasn't my favorite subject* or *One of my favorite children's books is entitled "A Hole Is to Dig."*

...

Begin with a question. A question is a frame. Questions show you where to direct your gaze. Rhetorical questions can seem contrived or manipulative, so use them sparingly. But a real question—something you really want to know about or wanted to know about when you began the journey that led to writing this article or poem or story—offers you energy and direction. Once it's asked, it demands action: Speculate. Imagine. Try to remember. Figure it out. Look it up. A question puts you in conversation with yourself.

All thought is conversation. I had a student years ago—smart and funny and unpretentious—who would think out loud about whatever topic was under discussion. She often started her comments with "I thought about this and I asked myself, 'Self, how do you feel about . . . ?'" What she was modeling in an amusingly overt way was something I imagine we all do—go to the inner consultant to find things out. Or as a therapist friend of mine put it, "Go to the person in you who knows." So, you might begin with a question on the topic you want to write about: How do I feel about privatizing water? Why do I care whether we paint these walls blue or yellow? What does the school board do? Why *did* I become a vegetarian? Whatever answer occurs to you, put it down. See what new questions that raises.

Once you've posed the question, you might find yourself responding not with a direct answer but with a thought that goes off at an oblique angle. On privatizing water, for instance, you might note,

> I never really paused to think about what "privatization" meant until I read about how hard a small town in Michigan fought to stop Pepsi from draining their waterways for water they could bottle and sell. Then I heard how Bolivians fought to regain the right to water as a public utility. Then I had to think about what "private" has come to mean. So I began to read around about it and found my way to *The Shock Doctrine* by Naomi Klein. I bought half a dozen copies of the book and gave them to people I thought might care. Because now I care a lot about what gets privatized and what we have to fight to hold in common.

Personalizing the question—thinking about when it first occurred to me to ask it—makes it easy to begin in story mode. Examples come to mind: a movie, a news report, a book. Then a recognition that what began for you has put you on a learning curve you'd like to take us on.

Questions beget more questions. *How do people live with chronic pain? When did the estrangement begin? Are there alternatives to plastic? What happens to a town after a wildfire?* Let the questions come. Give them their own paragraphs if you like. You don't have to organize those paragraphs yet—just let the questions multiply. They will likely get more specific. And they'll likely branch out in multiple directions. A question about privatizing water might open questions about who oversees the "public goods" our tax money pays for. Or about water rationing in drought-prone areas. Or about river pollution or chemical dumping or who lives downstream. Or about how you can be sure your water is free of contaminants. Or about fracking. A good question has many tributaries.

* * *

Begin with an imperative. *Don't look away* . . . or *Watch* . . . or *Imagine*. . . . or *Look! A fly is caught in that spiderweb.* Or simply *Come. Wait.* Stephen King's basic advice about an opening line is that, in one way or another, "It should say Listen. Come in here. You want to know about this." Imagine starting a suspense story or an account of survival in wartime with an imperative: *Don't go any further if you're afraid of fear*. Or *Wake up. Sleep is dangerous now.* Readers are challenged—dared, even—to consider what they're willing to know or undergo. They're reminded that they're embarking on a story that could spill over into real life in unpredictable ways. Try it: just pick an imperative verb (as I just did) and see what comes next.

* * *

Begin in the middle. I believe it was Zelda Fitzgerald who famously mused, "I missed the beginning, came in at the middle, and can't stay for the end, but somehow I must try to make sense of it all." It's a fair summary of your situation and mine. We began in the middle (the thought occurs to me to write "muddle" instead, but I digress). Things were already going on—a war was happening, new neighbors were moving in, a parent had just lost a job, it was the hottest summer on record. We devise ways to make sense of what's happening and how things happen with whatever information is available when we arrive.

So, start with a word like *Already* or *Despite* or a phrase like *It wasn't over* and find out what you're in the middle of. Or try a few opening sentences that place you smack in the middle of things: *We're in the thick of it now.* Or *The news cycle sounds like a spinning roulette wheel.* Or *New layers of complication keep coming.* Of course, if you begin in the middle, you will at some point need to backtrack or flash back or somehow provide the backstory. That might involve some interesting play with verb tenses as you move around in time—a topic we'll come to later. Beginning in the middle will also, very likely, lead you to reflections on time itself—how patterns of experience repeat themselves, how the past is present, how, as one poet put it, "the past keeps changing" or, as another poet mysteriously assured us, "All is always now."

* * *

Begin with a story. One way into story is through another story. Try beginning with a small parable or teaching tale, perhaps in the spirit of legendary rabbis who answer every question with "Let me tell you a little story." Begin with a three-sentence anecdote, or a remembered scene, or an item from last week's news that caught your eye: "Our neighbor's child appeared at the door yesterday in tears . . ." or "When she wanted something, our four-year-old would prepare a case before asking. I was sure she would grow up to be a lawyer. . . ." "Last week the *Times* ran a piece about a detention center near my home town. . . ." Stories, even very short ones, invite curiosity, speculation, and expectation. And if your opening story is a story within the larger story you're about to tell, we are led to read it and hold it on the assumption that it is significant. The meaning of what is about to unfold is somehow signaled or contained in the kernel of the opening paragraph.

* * *

Beginnings raise other kinds of questions. Whether, for instance to start with first, second, or third person: *I'm not sure why I'm telling you this. . . . You'll wonder why I'm telling you this. . . . She still wonders why I tell this story.* In Christa Wolf's *Patterns of Childhood* the writer tells her story in the first person to a "you" who is also herself about a "she" who is also herself. It's an interesting experiment in point of view as well as a compelling narrative.

As you begin, you'll have to address the question of narrative tense. Try a sentence out both ways and consider the tradeoffs: *They're arriving with their two children, a dog, and a gerbil.* Or *They arrived with their two children, a dog, and a gerbil.* Or *They had arrived with their two children, a dog, and a gerbil.*

* * *

Begin in time. All beginnings locate us, and some locate us primarily in time. We become aware that we've just stepped into a stream of ongoingness: something came before and something will come after. Even an account of the fall of the Roman Empire or the locust swarm in East Africa may begin with a moment when a small thing happened and something shifted. When you foreground the time dimension, you invite your reader to think about how things unfold or evolve or develop—how one thing seems to lead to another. The questions that are the basis of all narrative arise: *What happened next? What will happen next? What could happen next? What happened before that? What just happened?*

Moments are what we have. We may know what day or hour or era we are living in, but living happens in moments. One of Wendell Berry's poems ends with the simple statement, "What we need is here." Imagine how that applies to the moment in which you're sitting down to write. The moment you're in is sufficient—you don't have to wait for a stroke of insight or epiphany. You have what you need. Pick a remembered moment: *The sound of a newspaper landing on the porch the morning of . . . suddenly made me . . .*

You can:

Write *into* a moment—*As I watch the morning sun move across the table . . .*

Write *from* a moment—*The couple behind me had resumed their whispering . . .*

Write *about* a moment—*The look they exchanged as the phone rang stayed with me . . .*

Write *beyond* a moment—*Next month I'll see this encounter differently, no doubt . . .*

See what wants to happen next. Choose a word for the next sentence—*suddenly*, maybe, or *turning*. Now what?

* * *

Begin in space. Some beginnings locate us explicitly in space. Imagine, and invite your readers to imagine, a place where certain things are likely to happen, or particularly unlikely to happen, a place that evokes feelings as soon as it's mentioned, or a place that reminds them the person writing the sentence is a human being, somewhere on the planet, breathing and thinking.

You can:

Write *into* a place—*One stone doorway in the ruined castle remains intact . . .*

Write *from* a place—*I've been in this waiting room long enough to peruse two old issues of a magazine I'd never subscribe to . . .*

Write *about* a place—*Little has changed on this tree-lined street where my grandfather grew up, though he wouldn't recognize the city beyond his tidy neighborhood.*

Write *beyond* a place—*The few artifacts my mother brought back from her years in India make it real for me like no other place I've never been.*

...

Begin at the edge of nowhere. When you begin, you venture into the unknown. You can't and don't yet need to foresee . . .

how all the puzzle pieces go together
what accidents might change your trajectory
how you're going to get through this
who might become part of the story
what ideas will occur to you along the way

Not only when you write fiction or memoir, but even when you write an op-ed or reflective essay or a project proposal or play or poem, things will happen that you didn't plan for. Welcome them. Keep your outline or plan or list of talking points open-ended, with ample space for new thoughts or examples or scenes to occur. If you're not willing to be surprised—if you think you have to have an airtight, exquisitely detailed outline—you may succeed in delivering useful information, but what you write isn't likely to be evocative or provocative or enlightening. Make room for the Spirit to speak.

Because when you begin you don't yet know where you are. You have to be shown. Once you have a sentence or a paragraph, ask yourself . . .

What am I at the end of?
What have I been dropped into the middle of?
What am I at the beginning of?

That *what* is already there—the great course of human events you've stepped into. You're writing into and from a long conversation that began long before you were born and will continue after you die. Your story may begin in the middle of a family crisis or a move across the country. Your story is also being written in a time of climate change, wars, pending elections. The historical moment you occupy inevitably shapes your point of view, though your story is actually about how bricks were made in ancient Egypt. When I write, I'm situated in my own time and place. What I write about is situated in its time and place. The distance between them can be bridged. The boundaries between them are permeable.

* * *

We can't really do justice to beginnings without pausing over the paradoxes: that when we begin we're already in the middle, that we may be beginning because we've come to an end. "In my end is my beginning," Eliot wrote, quoting Mary, Queen of Scots and, doubtless, others. It's a repeated idea because it's true. The end of an episode or a scene or a day in the life, or—some of us believe—of life itself is a place of beginning. And it's true on more than one level: *end* can mean purpose. Our deepest purposes, not always perfectly conscious, lead us to the places where journeys begin. With that in mind, try one of these "concluding" sentences and see what begins:

I'm done with all that now . . .
Finally I see what it was for . . .
I'm cured.

Or imagine a final sentence that suggests a beginning. Consider (and write) the concluding paragraph that precedes it.

And so we begin.
And now, finally, I can start.
At last the door swings open.
The child I was is available to me now.
A new history may be what saves us.

Once you've tried these exercises, played with beginnings for a while, scan through them and pick your favorite. Before you conclude any writing session, it's a good practice to pick a few favorites—your favorite passage or sentence or image. Your favorite sentence for rhythm. Your favorite verb. The best way to learn from your own writing is to notice the good bits that give you particular pleasure and to notice the pleasure itself—the surge of energy that comes with an effective choice. The "joy of a graceful sentence." The more you notice them, the more they'll happen. Then back up a little and consider, as you look at what you've started . . .

what field of possibility your opening sentences open
how they establish a frame: where are we in time and space?
what you've let your reader know about the narrator
what you've invited, what you've foreclosed, what challenge you've offered your readers.
what tone they set: What might the reader already be feeling? Or hoping for?

• • •

Begin in hope. Beginning is an act of hope. It's also an act of faith—that this task is yours to undertake, that help or inspiration or ideas will keep coming, that you'll find the words you need. And it's an act of love—for the practice of writing, for what you're writing about, for those you may be writing it for whether you know them or not.

And yet, even as you begin with a heart full of hope and a pen full of ink (or a fully charged laptop), you don't yet know exactly what to hope for. Consider how T. S. Eliot's words apply to this moment of beginning: "I said to my soul, be still and wait without hope / for hope would be hope for the wrong thing." Ask yourself:

What do I hope for?
What might I need to stop hoping for in order to stay open to what comes?
What am I willing to allow for?

Do I hope this argument will change the mind of someone with the power to change policy? Do I hope my memoir will be as edgy and provocative as Mary Karr's or as daring as Sarah Aziza's? Or as inspirational as Cheryl Strayed's? Might I need to stop hoping to impress my readers so I can stay humbly focused on inviting them to notice or feel or rethink? What kinds of concessions, digressions, abbreviations, or impulsive interruptions can I afford to allow for when they occur to me? These questions are good ones to raise when you take a break and walk around the block or fold the laundry. They clear mental space. They keep you accountable.

. . .

Begin with prayer. If, like me, you believe your writing practice is a dimension of your spiritual practice, you might want to begin with a prayer to open the channel that connects you to the Spirit who guides and teaches and inspires and informs you. Simple prayers are good: *Let words come. Keep my ego from interfering. Help me notice. Let this become a gift for whoever it's for.* Or simply an act of gratitude: *Thank you for this time, space, equipment, desire, calling.* If, unlike me, you don't really think about writing that way, you might still find it helpful simply to clarify and speak your intention: *May my sentences be alive and authentic. May I trust and take delight in this process. May my words be blessings.*

MOVE THE CAMERA

I've always believed that photography is a way to shape human perception.

—James Balog

When I think of *The Scarlet Letter*, I see Hester Prynne in my mind's eye, emerging from the prison door, holding Pearl. I remember the scene as if I had been there, standing with the townspeople gathered to watch her walk of shame to the scaffold.

When I think of Chimamanda Ngozi Adichie's *Amerikanah*, I see an African woman sitting with African American women in a hair salon watching a hairdresser section and braid cornrows.

When I think of Barbara Kingsolver's *Prodigal Summer*, I see an old man and an old woman, tough, seasoned farmers, sparring with words over the fence that divides their farms.

What I imagine as I read—the structures, the spaces, the colors, the sounds of voices, the postures, the fine lines on faces or the quality of light—comes back to me as dream images do. I've been there. I've moved around those villages, farms, and city streets, or along the Appalachian Trail with Bill Bryson or through sultry Indian heat with Estha in Arundhati Roy's *The God of Small Things*.

My vision of Pemberley, of course, and of Elizabeth and Darcy, has been reshaped almost entirely by having watched the BBC version of *Pride and Prejudice* several times. Now Darcy, for me, will always be Colin Firth, and Jennifer Ehle's "fine eyes" are the ones I see when I return to the text. As for most of us now alive, my imagination has, for good or ill, been colonized by film. Increasingly sophisticated camera work has accustomed us all to the camera's-eye view, the quick shift from one angle to another, the way lighting and dolly shots and filters can deliver their own messages. The way time- and space-frames shift and keep reframing what we see.

* * *

Scene making, whether in fiction, nonfiction, or poetry, involves "camera work"—a visual metaphor that has helped me think about how to locate both narrator and reader in time and space. What you invite readers to see with the mind's eye depends on where you place the camera. Changing the vantage point now and then helps remind the reader that no one way of viewing an action or character is comprehensive.

Consider, for instance, how the camera moves in these two successive sentences:

> I walked in just as she was pulling heavy frying pans from a low cupboard. She prepared food with a kind of tenderness, forming patties and slicing vegetables with visible pleasure, handling each leaf of romaine as a shapely, satisfying thing worthy of its own moment of appreciation, as though, handling it, she was honoring the hands that had picked it under the hot Salinas sun.

Notice how the narrator calls our attention first to the larger visual features—the frying pan, the cupboard, the cook—and then to her hands and the foods she handles, then to the lettuce fields of a particular place. It's a simple move to narrow the frame and move in for a close-up; we do this kind of thing mostly unconsciously, but to do it consciously is to think a little more strategically about how little shifts of focus might add dimension or tension or ambiguity to a scene or character. Also notice that our attention is called first to the way the narrator sees, then to the way the cook sees, then to the hands of working people in the fields where the lettuce grew. These few sentences introduce several layers of awareness. "Camera work" can help us learn to imagine the "understory" of whatever we're looking at.

Let's imagine you're writing into your memoir a scene in a kitchen when, as a child, you dropped and broke a glass and your mother, afraid for your bare feet, told you sharply not to move. In addition to lines of dialogue: "Oh! I'm sorry, Mom!" "Don't move—you'll cut yourself"—you might call the reader's attention to the silence in the next room where an argument stopped when the glass broke. Or to the way the sun glittered on the shards of glass, making its own bit of magic. Or to a familiar, complicated look of annoyance and concern on your mother's face. Maybe all of these in succession. How the scene unfolds depends on where our attention is directed. Good camera work lets readers experience simultaneity even in successive sentences. The metaphor of the camera gives us a way to think about the inherent tension in writing between the linearity of a sentence and the all-at-onceness of a single moment in which emotions, events, memories, and connections happen, only later to be teased apart and recognized.

* * *

Let's look at a few examples of interesting "camera work" and consider what we can learn from them.

In *Under the Feet of Jesus* Helena María Viramontes gives us an intimate view of the daily life of a young girl who moves with her migrant family up the California Central Valley to work as a grape harvester. Few readers will have witnessed the particulars of that life up close or had occasion to imagine how a child of migrant workers might make sense of her family life, obligations, rights, or dreams. The short paragraph below gives us a close-up of Estrella at work in the field:

> The white light of the sun worked hard. Even the birds wavered on the crest of the heat waves. Under the leafy grapevines, the

> grapes hung heavy. She had readied the large rectangular sheet of newsprint paper over an even bed of tractor leveled soil, then placed the wooden frame to hold the paper down. Now, her basket beneath the bunches, Estrella pulled the vine, slit the crescent moon knife across the stem, and the cluster of grapes was guided to the basket below.

Notice how your eye is directed from the sun to the birds to the grapevines and grapes, zooming in and in so that we move from landscape to intimate space. Then we get a shot of the character placing a frame, pulling the vine, slitting the stem, guiding the grapes. Notice the time markers: ripe grapes and sun, tractor and leveled soil, which remind us of the season and the stage workers have reached in the grape harvest. Then we get the word *Now*, which again "zooms in" from the season to the moment when the girl's knife meets the stem, slices it, and releases grapes from the vine.

Even in this brief paragraph, Viramontes, writing about the lives of migrant workers in California vineyards, is teaching us to pause before passing by. As a Californian, I know how easy it is to see workers as part of the landscape as you whiz by those fields in an air-conditioned car at 70 miles per hour. Unless writers and artists and journalists show us close-ups like this one, our awareness of what a grape harvest requires of a worker can recede into comfortable unconsciousness. Close-ups keep us conscious, and sometimes, like this one, may awaken a drowsy conscience.

Before you go on, **try writing a paragraph** about someone engaged in work many don't notice—how the janitor cleans a vacated classroom; how a person on an assembly or inspection line in a factory keeps pace with the conveyor belt; how an apprentice construction worker stands in the sun regulating traffic on a blocked two-lane road.

* * *

Rudolfo Anaya's *Bless Me, Ultima* allows us a similarly intimate look at the life of a child of a Mexican American family in the rural Southwest. The story moves us around several settings—two households, the town, and the river that runs through it—against the broad backdrop of the *llano*, or grassy plain, beyond. These few sentences give us a sweeping look at this world from the eyes of the child, as remembered by the adult narrator:

> Around me the moonlight glittered on the pebbles of the llano, and in the night sky a million stars sparkled. Across the river I could see the twinkling lights of the town. In a week I would be returning to school, and as always I would be running up the goat path and crossing the bridge to go to church. Sometime in the future I would have to build my own dream out of those things that were so much a part of my childhood.

Notice the scope of the opening sentence in this paragraph. It's cosmic—earth and sky taken in at one long glance. The next sentence shifts from the long vertical focus and gives a broad horizontal view of river and town, bisected by the goat path and the bridge—two distinct lines on the sweeping canvas of dark and light. Then we see the school and the church—buildings that offer another kind of visual marker that, with the goat path and bridge, map the speaker's field of vision and awareness.

At the same time the time frame shifts from a moment to a week to sometime in the future, so space and time frames work in a kind of counterpoint: spatial awareness comes in closer, temporal awareness widens. Together the movement in this paragraph gives us a sense of the richness and complexity of the narrator's way of seeing and remembering. We are aware both of how he reconstructs this scene as a memory and of how he experienced it as a child—a double consciousness that is one of the most interesting features to work with in memoir writing. This beautiful novel is written in retrospect as a memoir by an older narrator but has a lot to teach about the uses, and pliability, of memory.

* * *

In a third scene, again from the point of view of a child, Willa Cather offers one of her many startling visual transitions. She takes us from an ordinary moment to a sense of place and time that is almost shockingly deep and mythic:

> I can remember exactly how the country looked to me as I walked beside my grandmother along the faint wagon-tracks on that early September morning. Perhaps the glide of long railway travel was still with me, for more than anything else I felt motion in the landscape; in the fresh, easy-blowing morning wind, and in the earth itself, as if the shaggy grass were a sort of loose hide, and underneath it herds of wild buffalo were galloping, galloping . . .
>
> Alone, I should never have found the garden—except, perhaps, for the big yellow pumpkins that lay about unprotected by their withering vines—and I felt very little interest in it when I got there. I wanted to walk straight on through the red grass and over the edge of the world, which could not be very far away. The light air about me told me that the world ended here: only the ground and sun and sky were left, and if one went a little farther there would be only sun and sky, and one would float off into them, like the tawny hawks which sailed over our heads making slow shadows on the grass. While grandmother took the pitchfork we found standing in one of the rows and dug potatoes, while I picked them up out of the soft brown earth and put them into the bag, I kept looking up at the hawks that were doing what I might so easily do.

Notice two time markers in the opening sentence: "I can remember" reminds us of the distance in time from which the adult narrator is portraying his younger self. "Early September" situates us in a season and climate and in the immediate experience of the younger self being portrayed.

The writer pays a lot of attention to horizontals in this passage—to the width and breadth of the earth, the rolling grassland, and to the stretch of wagon tracks and railroad across that wide space.

Then the focus shifts to a bounded space—the garden, and the pumpkins as distinct objects within the garden, and the withering vines that bring us close enough to sense their texture. It's worth noting that "withering" also serves as a time marker that conveys a stage in the season when the harvest is ready.

Those details offer a sharp contrast to the dreamscape of earth and sky and endless space. The hawks fly at the edge of the frame—at the boundary between the physical and imaginative worlds. We're brought back to Earth by their shadows, then the pitchfork, the potatoes, the dirt, and the bag. In this way, Cather deftly frames two states of consciousness: the here and now—the physical, visible world—and the realm of dream and possibility.

* * *

Keeping camera work in mind as you read, and later as you write, can help both you and your readers notice things it's easy to overlook. **As you read, ask:**

- From what distance in time or space is the reader, or the narrator, seeing the events, images, or characters? From across the street? From two feet away?
- How wide is the frame in a given paragraph? How might mention of the rising moon or a grasshopper widen or narrow the frame?
- How much does the focus vary?
- Where are the light and shadow? What colors are mentioned?
- What's in the foreground? The background?
- How is the space the paragraph takes on the page related to the space described? You can cover a wide landscape—the

Yorkshire moors if you're Emily Brontë or the Indian Ocean if you're Melville—in a few sentences. Or you can hold a long focus on a single fish in a stream, if you're Hemingway and Nick Adams has paused on a bridge to gaze into the water.

* * *

Experiment with your "camera eye":

Write a short scene that takes place inside a room while also making us aware of what's going on outside the room and why that might matter.

Write a short scene or paragraph where you make us aware of the "soundscape" by alluding to sounds—the permeability of the walls, for instance, or the rumbling of nearby trucks, or the wind on the grass in a nearby meadow. (As you explore these first two framing possibilities, you might look up Billy Collins's poem "Why I Don't Keep a Gun in the House" for inspiration. It's focused on a man in a room and a barking dog outside. Or imagine someone cowering in a room in Gaza or in Tehran while bombs fall nearby.)

Write an imaginative scene based on a known story like the parable of the prodigal son, for instance, giving us a sense of why "where" might matter, including colors, textures, distances, heat, light, etc. Take us from a spacious room to a pigsty to a dusty road at the end of which we can see a figure running, arms outstretched.

Write a series of single sentences that offer a distinct "camera angle" from which we might reframe a common experience of an event or place. For instance, a description that gives us the feel of being in a big-box store from the vantage point of a child, or of an empty church sanctuary from the vantage point of a cleaning woman. You might begin with signifying objects like the products on the bottom shelf or a mop leaning against a pew.

Write a few sentences that move us from a landscape view to a close-up or take us from a moment into a broad historical sweep of time. Remember Julie Andrews twirling on a hill surrounded by Alps, singing, "The hills are alive," and then standing before the mother superior by a small window in the stone wall of an ancient convent.

Write a few sentences that make us aware of air and light rather than of the objects in the visual field. Think of how the impressionist painters did this—how insistently they said, "See light! See color! See vibration! Nothing has sharp outlines around it. Everything is haloed."

* * *

Remember that when you write, you're a guide. You help your readers see in ways they may not be used to seeing. Sometimes you give them an inside view of something they wouldn't otherwise have access to. Sometimes, by changing the distance on something familiar, you invite them to see it in new terms—perhaps to recognize or complicate a few unexamined assumptions or judgments. There's always an ethical dimension to how we see what we see: frames—and frames of reference—inevitably exclude things. But we can shift the frames, widen them, use them to establish new vantage points and vanishing points. Helping readers reimagine and reframe might move someone from indifference toward engagement or, beyond that, to compassion. When that happens, everyone benefits.

DEVELOP AND DIGRESS

Sometimes you need to go in before you go on.

—Me, in a thousand workshops

"Tell me more." It's a generous invitation as well as a challenge: develop your point. My husband, a natural listener, experienced in pastoral care, has a lovely way of asking, "What was that like for you?" It's an open-ended question, gentle and welcoming, that also urges the storyteller to explore a memory for particulars, recognize feelings, find words that convey the quality of a moment or place. Words that suffice. Saying "a little more" makes the message matter a little more. Even an extra sentence says it was a thought worth hovering over before moving on.

Over the years, instead of writing an instruction like "Develop this point" in the margins of students' papers, I began to pose simple questions: How? Where? In what way? Against what odds? *Develop* isn't a self-explanatory verb. To do it is to answer any of the questions you could pose at any point in any story: Who, what, when, where, how, and, more complicatedly, why. Sometimes, if I asked them in person, the questions would make those who had hastened through the assignment squirm a little. Generalities come easy and cost little. Specifics take a bit more thought. Sometimes (gasp!) even a bit of research. How do you know? is a good development question.

* * *

Once you've written a sentence or two, you face a choice: Go on, or go in? Make your next point? Pause to muse about a word you just used? Offer a quick example? Tell a bit of backstory before proceeding? Qualify what you just said? Drop in a quote? Make a lateral move: "by the way," or "This reminds me of," or "Before we continue let's not forget . . ."?

Let's say you begin a story with a sentence like this:

The neighbors' dog has been barking all afternoon.

Imagine the possibilities that simple (albeit annoying) fact introduces:

This has happened for several days in a row.
I wonder if dogs always bark at something or just bark for no apparent reason.
There must be noise ordinances in this town.
I'm considering kidnapping that lonely creature; she's a victim of neglect.
I'm a goldfish person, myself.

Each of those sentences takes off in a different direction. A second sentence, like a second dot on a graph, sets up a line of development: you've now committed yourself to provide a little more history and context or to offer the fruits of your research on dog behavior or to move your thoughts toward noise pollution or the matter of responsible pet ownership or a bit of wry comedy. Your second sentence commits you to a path at least for the remainder of the opening paragraph, and perhaps for the whole story. The compass is now pointed in a direction.

* * *

Nothing just goes "on." Trains of thought run through hilly, circuitous landscapes. They go around, cut through, rise above, circle, and sometimes stop cold while repairs are being made. Once in a while, they turn at signs marked "by the way" or "moreover" or "nevertheless" or "on the other hand." Then they circle back with, "Still, . . ."

* * *

We all learned in some English class to "develop" our points—basically to say more about what we put out there as a main idea. To develop a line of argument, a character, a scene, a paragraph, you generally do one of these:

define key terms (*and to me, what "excellence" means is . . .*)
offer a little etymology (*oddly, "taxes" and "taxonomy" come from the same root . . .*)
trace causes and effects (*here's what happens when bee populations die . . .*)
point out implications (*suggesting people "make better choices" about food implies that they have a choice to begin with . . .*)
offer specific examples (*children can share responsibility by feeding the dog, for instance . . .*)
offer contrasts (*the less punitive prison system in Norway leads to lower recidivism rates than in the United States . . .*)
trace a bit of history (*automatic weapons changed warfare . . .*)
give some immediate context (*the phone rang just as the birthday girl was blowing out candles . . .*)
pursue hypotheticals (*if they hadn't gone to the beach that day . . .*)

Most importantly, developing anything—an argument, a scene, a lyrical moment—means moving your reader deftly, smoothly, sometimes forcefully or disruptively from *what's happening* to *how* and *why*. It's been surprising to me over years of reading undergraduate essays how many can give a perfectly intelligent, even compelling, account of *what*—describing, observing, detailing—without ever getting to *how* or *why*. Description or summary or paraphrase at its best can be compelling, but it is not analysis. Nor is it story.

The basic arc of development (and this applies to the long arc of a story or argument and the short arc of a paragraph, or even a sentence) generally travels from *what* we're being invited to consider or imagine to *how* it works, *how* it's laid out, *how* it's related to other objects, stories, or events, to *why* it might be important. For example, the arc might be something like *This is a story about a man who was wrongly convicted of a crime, put on death row, and ultimately exonerated. Here's how he landed in the wrong place at the wrong time and ended up in court. Here's how the lawyers argued and how the judge and jury ended up with their judgments. Here's why it might matter to hear this story now, in an age of mass incarceration.*

Of course, these questions aren't generally addressed in strict sequence. And along the way you'll find places to elaborate on *who* and *when* and *where*. In a biography, the *who* might remain in the foreground most of the time, though never independently of the others. If you think of each of these question words as a dimension or layer of the story, you'll begin to notice where you may need to shift focus from one of them to another for a paragraph or sentence, and to broaden your lines of development. Here's an exercise: try a simple version of a story you have to tell. In any order that appeals to you . . .

Say *what*
Say *who*
Say *how*
Say *where*
Say *when*
Say (or at least imply) *why*

Move the parts around as you will. You can start with *how* and *who* and turn a corner into *what* and let us speculate about *why* until you reveal it at the end. Or you can start with *where* and spend a whole paragraph (or several, if you're George Eliot) telling us where—what hills, whose croft, which barn—before peopling your landscape with characters. One way or another, though, you need to address if not fully answer these questions:

- *What happened?* (Possibly several things . . . an earthquake, a birth, an argument, an unexpected check in the mail.)
- *How did it happen?* (This could get large, depending on who's to be credited or who's clearly to blame, what their father did to them, whether they were drunk at the time, how the stock market crash affected their moods and fortunes, what delayed them on the way home . . .)
- *Who made it happen?* (Hardly ever just one person. Sometimes God. Or the devil. Or, more likely, a well-intentioned but misguided human who realized their costly mistake belatedly and spent the rest of the story making amends . . .)
- *To whom did it happen?* (Usually to our hapless—or happy—protagonist, but often to their whole family, their jealous sister, their erstwhile best friend, the children they ultimately had . . .)
- *When did it happen?* (Last week, last month, when the rains came, a century ago when their immigrant grandfather made a life-changing decision . . .)
- *Where did it happen?* (Down by the pond, at the edge of a quiet town, under a particular tree, under the stars, on a battlefield or in an emergency room or a classroom or a cave . . .)
- *Why? Why then? Why there?* (Because social, psychological, economic, spiritual forces were at work in ways we shall take the remaining two hundred pages to trace.)

As you see, the answers to any of these questions are rife with possibility. They lead in multiple directions. They overlap. Causality is never singular and often hard to trace. If all you learn from reading and writing stories and poems is that there are always multiple points of view, ways of telling, identifiable causes, and possible outcomes, you will have become, I believe, a more imaginative, open-minded, compassionate person. As it happens, I also believe we need to keep learning those lessons—hence the continual making of stories from one generation to the next. Literary theorist Georges Polti may have somehow been right when he oddly claimed there are only thirty-six plots (or "dramatic situations" as he called them), but, like the twenty-six letters of the English alphabet, a lot can be done with those plots. They can be developed in countless ways. So here are a few thoughts—or rules of thumb—my thumb—about development:

* * *

Somewhere in the process of development, you're likely to digress. I hope you do. Something will occur to you that's a little to one side—a comparison or a pertinent memory or an odd one-off thought whose relationship to what you're setting out to say may seem questionably tangential. Pay attention to those occurrences. They are your writing muse giving you permission to stop marching onward, start strolling, and notice what "comes up." See what's in your peripheral vision or in the rearview mirror. You might, for instance . . .

Take a small detour: Go a bit off topic, with some assurance that it will become clear why you're doing so.

Shift narrative stance: offer an aside, for instance. (*And here, dear reader, is where the course of history changed.*)

Shift the spotlight to a minor detail or character for a sentence or two. (*As tempers and voices rose, the waiting souffle quietly fell.*)

Tell a tangential story. (*It was not unlike a situation her mother had often told about, laughing at her own folly.*)

Widen or narrow the frame. (*She couldn't keep her eye from straying to the fly making its way across the salad.*)

* * *

A digression might begin with . . .

And by the way . . .
This, of course, reminds me of . . .
As I write this, I realize . . .
None of this was actually on his mind, though . . .
But wait . . . !
This is a sorrowful fact.

In most cases, digression isn't a distraction, but rather an essential characteristic of human thought, which is multifaceted, nodal, cross-referential, and mercurial. Historians, journalists, and storytellers speak about the "rabbit trails" they could or do pursue before returning to the "main road." Occasionally they mark the end of these little excursions with a brief, wry "But I digress."

* * *

Consider how the digressive sentences in this passage from Jill Lepore's *These Truths: A History of the United States* contribute to overall enlargement and development of her point about what history is. Notice where sentences or clauses or phrases angle away from the main subject.

> History isn't only a subject; it's also a method. My method is, generally, to let the dead speak for themselves. I've pressed their words between these pages, like flowers, for their beauty, or like insects, for their hideousness. The work of the historian is not the work of the critic or of the moralist; it is the work of the sleuth and the storyteller, the philosopher and the scientist, the keeper of tales, the sayer of sooth, the teller of truth.

Notice how Lepore reframes the question "What is history?" to invite us to consider how history is made: it's not a noun, but a verb, a process. Then she lets us in on her method. But before going on to elaborate on her method, she plays with metaphors and analogies and moves us from thinking literally about how she handles documents to thinking imaginatively and comparatively in ways that may reframe our notions of history and historians.

> **Try this:** Develop a paragraph addressing a common misconception or oversimplification of something you know well. Offer a corrective, helping people imagine how it really is. Try imitating Lepore, starting, for instance, with something whose complexities you'd like to recognize: Biology isn't only a field of study; for some it's a path to self-understanding. Or knitting isn't only a hobby; it's a way of opening space for rumination. Or cooking isn't only a necessity; it's a way of loving the people you love.

• • •

Annie Dillard, a delightfully digressive writer, gives us this account of how she began her book *Pilgrim at Tinker Creek.* Notice how many times she redirects our attention for the space of a sentence or two before returning to the main focus, which is how she came to embark on her book.

> In October, 1972, camping in Acadia National Park on the Maine coast, I read a nature book. I had very much admired this writer's previous book. The new book was tired. Everything in it was the dear old familiar this and the dear old familiar that. God save us from meditations. What on earth had happened to this man? Decades had happened, that was all. Exhaustedly, he wondered how fireflies made their light. I knew—at least I happened to know—that two enzymes called luciferin and luciferase combined to make the light. It seemed that if the writer did not know, he should have learned. Perhaps, I thought that night reading in the tent, I might write about the world before I got tired of it.
>
> I had recently read Colette's *Break of Day,* a book about her daily life that shocked young metaphysical me by its frivolity: lots of pretty meals and roguish conversations. Still, I read it all; its

vivid foreignness intrigued me. Maybe my daily life would interest people by its foreignness, too. And was it at that time that I read Edwin Muir's wonderful *Autobiography* and noticed how much stronger was the half he wrote when he was young?

A *New Yorker* essay that fall noted that mathematicians do good work while they are young because as they age they suffer "the failure of the nerve for excellence." The phrase struck me, and I wrote it down. Nerve had never been a problem; excellence sounded novel.

How boldly committed to ideas we are in our twenties! Why not write some sort of nature book—say, a theodicy? In November, back in Virginia, I fooled around with the idea and started filling out five-by-seven index cards with notes from years of reading.

Notice Dillard's time and space markers. The first sentence gives us date and place. Then the phrase "Decades had happened" gives us a sense of the time lapse between the writing of the book she's reading and her reading it. Then she brings us back to the present moment "at night, in the tent," then to the season, "that fall." Finally, we end up "back in Virginia" where she gathers thoughts from "years of reading." All these mentions of moments or periods of time create a sense of how experiences are layered on one another, how moments intersect. The sequence of events that led to her writing her book gives way to a more interesting sense of how it all came about, how one thing connected with another, not necessarily leading to it, but surfacing and converging.

Try this: Using Dillard as a model, write about how it came about that you took up a project. Let your sentences take us to different events that connected in ways you might not have anticipated or even recognized at the time.

* * *

Let's look at one final example of purposeful digression. In *Neither Here Nor There*, one of his several quirky, entertaining travel narratives, Bill Bryson recounts a short stay at a favorite European hotel. His account becomes more a testimony to his own capacious curiosity than a story about his time in the hotel:

> Fifteen minutes later, I was in a room at the Hôtel Adolphe Sax, lying on the bed with my shoes on (disintegrating into a hermitic slobbiness is one of the incidental pleasures of solitary travel), breaking my teeth on the Toblerone, and watching some daytime television offering on BBC-1—a panel discussion involving people who were impotent or from Wolverhampton or suffering some other personal catastrophe, the precise nature of which eludes me now—and in half an hour was feeling sufficiently refreshed to venture out into Brussels. I always stay in the Adolphe Sax because it gets BBC-1 on the TV and because the elevators are so interesting, a consideration that I was reminded of now as I stood in the corridor beside an illuminated DOWN button, passing the time, as one does, by humming the "Waiting for an Elevator Song" ("Doo dee doo dee doo dee doo doo"), looking speculatively at my neck in the mirror, and wondering idly why hotel hallway carpet is always so ugly.

The forward movement of the passage takes us from his arrival in a hotel room through a short rest for watching TV, out to the hall where he's waiting for an elevator. But those happenings are backgrounded to the movement of his agile mind, both then and now—what he noticed, felt, wondered, what he now thinks about what he did and felt then. The apparent irrelevancies—keeping his shoes on, the sensation of biting on hard chocolate, the look of his neck in the mirror, the ugly carpet—are, in fact, what we come to take an unexpected interest in. He is teaching us how, in unpredictable ways, everything is connected: nothing is utterly irrelevant or insignificant in a lived moment. What we notice in peripheral vision may turn out to be important in ways we couldn't foresee or even identify until we see, in retrospect, how small things come to matter. Much of Bryson's writing is as much about the pleasure of the active, observant, curious mind itself as about the places he visits.

Try this: Write a paragraph about arriving someplace and settling in that gives a similar account of what it felt like, what you noticed, how a memory intruded, or a sound outside, or a feeling or sensation evoked by something your eye happened to fall upon. Be as playful as possible. See where it takes you.

* * *

Here are a few more prompts for practice. Remember, what you're practicing here is purposeful (not pointless) digression—small detours that are one of the pleasures of a curious soul with an appetite for finding out what more might be seen just off the beaten path, what may lurk in the forest, whether there are edible mushrooms or actual fairies, what more life may have to offer.

Try this: Develop one of these sentences (or one of your own) for four or five more sentences, including a briefly digressive observation:

The school year will be starting soon.
Efforts to improve public school lunches appear to be stalled.
Sometimes you have to let an argument end in a stalemate.
She pulled into his driveway and wondered what to do next.

* * *

Remember, as you think about the pleasures and purposes of digression, that a straight line may be the shortest distance from one point to another, but it's probably also the most boring way to get there.

DO THE WORD WORK

The common word exact without vulgarity,
The formal word precise but not pedantic . . .

—T. S. Eliot

"What do you mean?" is one of the most exhilarating, challenging, interesting questions you can be asked. Immediately, if you accept the challenge, you start looking for new ways of putting a thought you had assumed was clear enough. How else might it be said? What metaphors or illustrations or modification might enable this particular person to understand it better? I've spent most of my professional life teaching college students and adults, but for one brief puzzling moment I found myself substitute teaching in a classroom full of squirrelly second-graders. I had my own children at that point and thought I knew how to talk with children. I certainly knew how to talk with mine. But that didn't mean I knew what to do standing in front of twenty-five of them, most in their desks, a few playing hangman at the blackboard, one wandering, and as I learned, prone to wander, bemused by the whole situation. Coming from children that age, "What do you mean?" is a particularly challenging question. Translating adult ideas or experiences into terms a seven-year-old can grasp requires a pause, a deep breath, and a moment to recall what it's like to be seven—smart, perhaps, but inexperienced. Children that age are still acquiring words and learning how to use them. And their contexts are limited. We build bridges out of words, hoping to help them get from inarticulate wonder or dismay to sentences that meet their needs.

* * *

If you're going to write in a way that's satisfying, you have to deepen, widen, complicate, and enliven your relationship with words. You may want to write in a way that underscores your authority and demonstrates your command of professional terminology. Or you may want to write simply and colloquially—in a down-home, accessible manner—unpretentious and appealing to the most cursory or hurried reader. Even then you can't just rely on the words you use every day, and if you want to be any good at it, you can't just use those words the way you use kitchen utensils. Words are indeed tools, but they're so much more. They're surgical instruments, musical instruments, spell-casters, lifelines, packets of energy that create their own magnetic fields, nodes in a fungal network that connects us to everyone on Earth and to our ancestors and to God.

I've written several other books about words that focus on what it takes to care for them in a culture where they're all-too-often flattened and battered and twisted, made to disguise the truth rather than serve it. I've also written about what can happen when you pause over a word or phrase, ponder it, look up its history, pay attention to associations that come with it, reframe it and share it in lines that make it new. I deeply believe words can be channels of healing and grace. They can have a sacramental character: they can help bring into being the things they name. I didn't invent this mystical view of language; these beliefs informed cultures of the ancient world, not because those cultures were "primitive," but because they lived closer to what some have called "original energies." Language has always been recognized as an instrument of transformation—of magic or healing or prayer. I won't repeat at length what I said in those books of mine (most of which are still around, and I encourage you to hasten out and buy them). But I will enumerate briefly here some of the kinds of "word work" we need to be doing as writers. Here's a partial list:

- **Love words**—Hang around them. Notice them. Keep learning new ones. Move them around. Enjoy what they do, not just what they say.
- **Tell the truth**—Not as obvious a task as it used to be, since various forms of propaganda including advertising have normalized half-truths, "spun" messages, and sometimes outright lies. Sometimes we have to tell truth slant to bring it back into visibility. Always we have to recognize we can't tell it "whole," since we're limited human creatures. But we can be clear with ourselves and our readers what we're trying to be faithful to.
- **Define as you go along**—Pause now and then to point out how meanings may have changed, how meanings may be multiple, what you mean when you use a word like *justice* or *costly* or *normal* or, say, *awesome*.
- **Care about precision**—Precise isn't the same as literal: a metaphor may give a sharper, clearer sense of what you mean than a technically appropriate but abstract descriptor. Precise language avoids abstraction. If you care about it you won't say "The bomb left destruction in its wake" but rather "The bomb left concrete rubble, burning cars, scattered vegetables from food stands, stray scarves, kitchen pots, and teddy bears on streets where survivors wandered, bewildered and afraid." It often takes longer to be precise, but not always. A similar statement of fact could be "The bomb destroyed a third of the buildings and two-thirds of the civilians in the city." We need to be willing to imagine what we're talking about in cases like these. Hard truths are too often hidden behind abstractions.
- **Don't tolerate lies**—The flip side of telling the truth: call out lies when you know that's what they are. Don't contribute to

normalizing them. Correct the record when you can. Beg to differ (or insist on it).

- **Read well**—Notice and notice—what writers do, how they do what they do, where they touch you or energize you or give you pause. Notice word choices and sentence structures and figures of speech, and notice where and how those things make a difference.
- **Stay in conversation**—It's like jazz performance. You hear the music differently each time. The give-and-take of conversation is improv; it keeps us in the moment, finding words to fit the occasion, waiting for the next serve as we prepare to hit the ball back from anywhere on the court.
- **Share stories**—It's one of the most ancient of human activities—probably as old as sex and eating. Other people's stories help us stretch into, reconsider, and reimagine our own. Stories help us recognize there are other paths through the forest, some of them worth exploring, some of them leading into thorns and thickets. Also, stories help us see how very alike we are in our needs, desires, delights, and hopes.
- **Love the long sentence**—Not in every paragraph, but now and then there's a place for a sentence that keeps saying we're not done yet—there's more—more layers, more mitigating factors, more implications. Especially when we've become so used to sound bites and texts, an occasional long sentence can reinvigorate the mind and spirit like a long run.
- **Mind your metaphors**—And other figures of speech. Metaphors matter more than most. They thread the world together: one thing is oddly like another. Pointing that out makes us notice something new about both things. Also about paradox. The woman's teeth really are and really aren't like pearls. The exiting crowd was and also wasn't a surging sea. Notice when verbs and common expressions have metaphorical implications: *They wanted to squeeze every drop of pleasure from their one evening.*

- **Practice poetry**—Even if you write prose. Even if you never show it to anyone—though I hope you do. There's a chapter about this later. Poetry is essential word work. Seeing what a phrase or line can do before it grows up to become a sentence is an important dimension of effective sentence-making.
- **Attend to translation**—Not just from one language to another, though if you do speak more than one language, it's good to use it or at least allude to it, perhaps borrow a word or phrase here and there, and call our attention to the fact that other people may actually think and speak in ways that might enrich us. Also, attend to the ways we translate every time someone says, "What do you mean?" Pay attention to how you translate a complex idea for a child or a layperson who doesn't have your training. How you simplify without dumbing down.
- **Borrow and steal**—Pick up new words and phrases, new usages, where you can. Allude to old ones. Dust off antique terms now and then and reintroduce them to the surprise and delight of readers. Imitate unabashedly and thank the people worth imitating. Remember that as a writer you're a participant and member in a long lineage and wide fellowship of word workers bound together by love of language. Share the wealth as they have.
- **Play**—There's a whole chapter on this later, too. Playfulness is an essential habit of mind for a writer—a sign of spiritual health and, paradoxically, of maturity. That you can afford to be playful even about highly serious things suggests that you live in trust that what you need will be given. If you're open to it, it will.
- **Pray**—It may seem odd to think of this as "word work," but putting our deepest longings, doubts, gratitude, and hope into words actually forges a living connection to the life force from which the first, truest words came.
- **Cherish silence**—Leave space around your words, spoken

and written. Notice what those spaces allow for and open up. Notice what germinates there. Notice what comes to you in silence that could only come in the absence of noise.

That's a bit of what I have to say about our work as stewards of language. Maybe you don't have to hasten out and buy my other books. But you might want to take a peek. I had a good time writing them.

* * *

Before we leave the general (and potentially endless) topic of word work, I want to spend a little time on a dimension of it that seems especially urgent, given the current state of public discourse. All of us who write and speak in public need to pay attention to the challenge of "loaded" language—language that triggers knee-jerk responses, usually fraught with emotion, and, as soon as it's spoken, tends to derail efforts at shared deliberation. As soon as you say "undocumented immigrant," for instance, or "reproductive rights" or "family values," or names like Netanyahu or Mother Teresa or Donald Trump, you're likely to set off a cascade of reactions that, spoken or unspoken, will make calm, detached reflection difficult.

Some words we may simply have heard repeated too often, too predictably. We tune out, thinking we've already heard all we need or want to hear on the subject. We may have heard one too many motivational talks on *team building*, for instance, or so many repeated instructions about what to do in the event of a water landing, we don't hear them anymore.

Some are hot-button words that occur daily in public conversation—newscasts, political speeches, motivational talks, podcasts. A lot of words are loaded in ways we can't fully anticipate. A word like *mother* or *father* might be loaded for someone who has suffered abuse from a parent, or a word like *boy* if someone has heard it used to humiliate him, or a word like *normal*, if it's applied to something that to the listener isn't normal at all, but a mark of privilege.

Loaded language is often predicated on a logical fallacy—"straw-man building," for instance, describes what one opposes in terms that reinforce a certain group's assumptions and make it easier to dismiss the opposition. The terms "fake news," for instance, or "liberal media" are themselves barriers to deeper inquiry about sources and framing of the news in question.

Another common fallacy behind much loaded language, especially in the United States with our history of two parties and polarized rhetoric, is the "false dichotomy," which presents a problem as an oversimplified either-or proposition without acknowledging that any middle ground is possible, as in terms like "the right side of history" or "with us or against us" or simply "the other side."

Rather than go through an extensive list of logical fallacies here, I'll suggest you look up such a list, readily available online, and see if you can find loaded language that offers examples of each fallacy—*hasty generalization*, *ad hominem*, *bandwagon*, and so on. It makes a good parlor game for a late evening with beer and a few word-nerdy friends.

The goal isn't to avoid loaded language; that's impossible. Even if you know a word is a trigger, you may have need of it to name or clarify what needs to be talked about. The challenge is to use words in such a way as to keep readers reading, keep listeners listening, and forestall snap judgments. Our job is to tell stories or describe events or situations in ways that keep reminding our readers that whatever human situation is at issue, it's not that simple. Our job is to move people beyond slogans and labels and sentences that begin with "It all really comes down to . . ." or "It's really just a matter of . . ." or (one of my pet peeves) "Either . . . or . . ." That last is vexing since there are far more than two sides to any question worth pondering. Even if the final judgment involves a binary choice, there are many factors to consider in, say, gun control legislation or border protection or how to fund public services or label public restrooms.

* * *

Let's consider a few strategies for speaking or writing in ways that may help people stay engaged and consider new perspectives on controversial matters that are hard even to name, since the language around them has become so riddled with highly charged associations:

1. Let the definition precede the term. In a sentence that starts not with the clearly loaded term but with a phrase that defines it, your reader has a moment to register your intention or context or meaning and conjure an image an instant before hearing the dreaded buzzword. Consider the order of this sentence, for instance: *Those whose position in this debate has been informed by personal suffering, parents who have lost children, deserve to be listened to on the matter of gun control legislation.* It's a small delay, but the fact that the term *gun control legislation* comes at the end of the sentence rather than at the beginning means your reader has a moment to imagine those parents before reacting to a term that may in itself elicit a quick conditioned response.

Try this: Reword these sentences so that the most-loaded term comes last after a phrase or two that may help complicate the reader's reaction to the term:

Abortion continues to be a point of major contention in ways that get oversimplified.
Factory farms are places meat-eaters should visit or at least read about before deciding where to buy meat and how much of it to eat.
White privilege is sometimes hard for white people to identify because it's the water they swim in.

The principle applies, of course, to paragraphs, where the most controversial terms might follow several sentences of reflection.

2. Pause for a bit of metaconversation—conversation about the conversation. Pause before using the word or phrase to acknowledge that it's loaded or problematic, that it's one people tend to react strongly to, that it's a word or phrase some people find offensive, or that it's a word or phrase that needs a little definition before we can have the conversation we need to have. Before introducing an anecdote about an *undocumented immigrant*, for instance, you might pause for a sentence or two to remind readers that *undocumented* doesn't always mean *illegal*—that documentation takes time and can be hard to get or keep, especially for people fleeing immediate threats. Or you might give a sentence to distinguishing between *immigrant* and *refugee*. Or you might pause to tell a brief story about someone who crossed a border in circumstances that made it hard to go through legal channels.

> **Try this:** Write a sentence or two of metaconversation about a loaded term that takes it on squarely with either a definition or an illustration or a gentle musing, for instance, *I wonder what comes up for any of us who concern ourselves with what happens at the borders.*

3. Decontextualize. The easiest way to lift the word out of the muddy swamp of bad feelings or the oversimplifications that run conversation into dead ends is to lift it out of its contemporary context and set it down in a different time zone. Or vice versa—to retrieve it from the antiques in the attic, dust it off, and use it. *When Shakespeare (or Jane Austen or Wilfred Owen) said "honor," it meant something a bit different from what it may mean to people now. North Americans tend to hear this word quite differently from the way English speakers in the former British Empire hear it.* Some, now, may be unable to hear it without irony. For some the word is hopelessly antique, or relevant only to military rhetoric. I've found myself reclaiming it when I say as an adult class draws to a close, "I'm going to finish here because I want to honor your time"; the word feels

good and refreshing to me because it lifts me out of current conventionalities just for a moment.

In the same way, a buzzword like *politically correct*, so often used to dismiss a position as mere posturing, may be heard a bit differently in the context of another generation's choices: *Being a pacifist during World War II was certainly not politically correct, and often met with bitter criticism or worse, but for some it was the only choice compatible with a deeply formed conscience.*

4. Frame it with a question. It helps me to get needed distance on a word I've come to hear as a mere buzzword if I frame it to myself or others as a question: *What, I wonder, did the term "liberal" mean to my parents, or my grandparents, or to Emily Dickinson or George Washington?* Or *I need to pause and consider, what are conservatives hoping to conserve?* Or *What's happening upstream from the people we've been calling lazy or indigent?* In each case a question may be a strategic way of introducing the metaconversation. It's best, of course, if the question is real, not simply rhetorical—if we can get ourselves to where we really do wonder and would like to hear the answer. A real question that invites a real answer is sometimes an act of courage. Because here's the thing about navigating the choppy waters of loaded language: No matter how beautifully, persuasively, or gracefully you write, if you write frankly and honestly about things that matter to you, you're going to piss somebody off. If we speak in public, we have to run that risk and toughen up enough to stay in the fray.

* * *

Before we conclude this chapter, let's review the characteristics of loaded language:

It serves as code or an identifier for a particular group.
It elicits a reactive emotional response.
Its emotive meaning doesn't always correspond to its historical meaning.

It bypasses (or attempts to bypass) thoughtful debate.
It perpetuates stereotypes.
It evolves in response to cultural shifts ("neutral" words acquire new meanings).
It often sensationalizes.
It sometimes sets up false dichotomies.
It appears in tabloid propaganda but also in poetry.
It includes buzzwords, words intended to classify and dismiss.
It includes words that "virtue signal"—show you belong to the right group.

See what terms you might add to this short list of ten loaded words and consider how you hear them:

freedom
family values
terror/terrorist
patriot/enemy
conspiracy
feminist
patriarchy
privilege
racist
biblical

Try this: Write a few sentences about your own response to any of these historically loaded phrases:

final solution
lone gunman
illegal immigrant
equal rights

tough on crime
defending our country
voter suppression

For your own future reference, keep a list of "loaded" words that trigger strong feelings and memories. Notice how these register in your body. These might be place names; names of particular objects you associate with occasions or a person; verbs that recall a way of moving or acting. Write a line or sentence linking the sensation with the word.

Try this: Read through these two excerpts, tag the loaded terms, and either respond to the way they're used or see if there are ways to reword sentences that deliver similar observations in a tonally different way.

From the New York Times

RALEIGH, N.C. — Clinic by clinic, county by county and up to the highest levels of state government, no state embodies the nation's post-Roe upheaval like North Carolina. In the eight months since the federal right to abortion was eliminated, leaving states free to make their own abortion laws, North Carolina, where the procedure remains legal up to 20 weeks, has become a top destination for people from states where it is banned or severely restricted. North Carolina experienced a 37 percent jump in abortions, according to WeCount, an abortion-tracking project sponsored by the Society for Family Planning, which supports abortion rights. Providers in the state performed 3,190 abortions in April 2022. That number soared to 4,360 in August, after Roe fell. It was the biggest percentage increase in any state.

From the Christian Century

The president of the Lutheran Church–Missouri Synod has called for the excommunication of unrepentant White supremacists in the church's ranks, rebuking an extremist effort to exert influence within the conservative Lutheran denomination.

In a letter dated February 21, LCMS President Matthew Harrison said he was "shocked to learn recently that a few members of LCMS congregations have been propagating radical and unchristian 'alt-right' views via Twitter and other social media." He noted far-right members were causing "local disruption" for congregations and alleged that LCMS leadership and deaconesses had fallen victim to online threats, some of which he described as "serious."

"This is evil. We condemn it in the name of Christ," Harrison wrote.

Harrison went on to rebuke the "horrible and racist teachings of the so-called 'alt-right,'" listing ideologies such as "white supremacy, Nazism, pro-slavery, anti-interracial marriage, women as property, fascism, death for homosexuals, even genocide."

* * *

You can't unload language. It carries whatever load we put on it as we turn it to our various purposes. But you can stay alert to the way you react to certain terms, the ways others do, the ways those terms are spun and traded on in public to produce an effect. You can gently, consistently, persistently retrieve words from partisan colonization by lifting them up, showing them off from new angles, and setting them down in new places. For writers writing now, it's a daily challenge.

FIND OUT WHO'S THERE

She wasn't doing a thing that I could see, except standing there leaning on the balcony railing, holding the universe together.

—J. D. Salinger

Literary portraiture is an art unto itself. Good character description can serve important social purposes: it can help us imagine others in ways that honor their complexity and foster compassion. I remember, for example, writing a long piece about my father in a journal workshop I attended. Dad wasn't mean—he was funny and imaginative and curious about the world, but he also had minimal capacity to empathize. He rarely spoke in terms of feelings—his or mine. He might have been "on the spectrum," but we had no access to such diagnostic terms at the time. Writing about him, though, staying with the task for more pages than I imagined when I grudgingly undertook the assignment, opened up my imagination for what it might be like to be him—limited, brilliant, misunderstood, wistful, bewildered about others' responses to him. It didn't change him, but it changed me. I was able to love him more, and differently.

Even if the story you're telling is primarily about your own journey, you'll be telling stories, directly or indirectly, about other people—about your mother, your colleagues, your self-absorbed client, your saintly neighbor, public figures about whom you have strong opinions. Sometimes you'll write about whole groups of people—academics, churchgoers, high-tech thirty-somethings, unhoused people, hospice patients, immigrants. You may write from the vantage point of an intimate witness, a participant, an observer, a constituent or parishioner or advocate or victim or critic.

Sometimes you'll write as a survivor. Most of us will at some point write someone's obituary or a eulogy. I was touched and surprised when my brother and I wrote independent reflections about our mother for her funeral at how they converged on very particular details—the way she used her capable hands; the way she laughed with her whole self; the way she dropped into the lives of suffering people with skilled, practical, unpretentious care; the way her deep faith expressed itself in ordinary acts of love for those given to her—students, strangers, family, friends, and all the small creatures who inhabited her beloved garden. It's a good assignment to write about someone you love, living or dead. In the process of finding words, I've learned, new tributaries of that love open and flow.

One way or another, you will write about other people. You have a right to write about them. We're all objects of interest in someone else's field of vision, and they get to go home and tell stories about meeting us in the grocery line or about what we said at a department meeting or about the nervous habits we thought no one noticed. We're all characters in someone's story. But you also have responsibilities to the people you write about: not to do harm, to respect their privacy, to honor the complexities of their lives and situations.

In this chapter we'll look at some features of literary portraiture that may help you consider ways to depict other people more ethically and effectively, inviting readers to imagine them with more nuance and compassion. We'll look at a few brief portraits in fiction and nonfiction and consider how writers make characters come alive.

* * *

Let's begin with these questions—good ones to ask yourself as you set out to describe a living person and even if you're creating a fictional character. They're not simply about craft but are pertinent ethical questions. Writing is never ethically neutral. Your choices will affect readers in real lives in real time.

- With what kind of authority or permission am I writing about this person?
- For what purpose(s)?
- How am I honoring the ambiguities and complexities of this character? Am I enabling readers to imagine that this person has a rich interior life? Conscience? Conflicts? A history that explains their behaviors?
- If there's humor in the portrayal, is it at the person's expense? Or at the expense of a group or type they represent?
- What archetypes am I drawing on in my portrayal?
- How am I inviting readers to admire, judge, identify with, or reimagine this person?
- What do I hope my readers learn or appreciate?
- What does it mean to do justice to the person being represented, even if they were or are abusive, corrupt, or have betrayed public or private trust?
- How does description of the body, physical environment, forms of speech or habits point toward deeper truths about the person?
- What if I'm writing about the person as part of my story, but disclosing things they might not choose to tell? Are there legal implications to disclosure?
- How may portraiture raise valuable questions about notions of beauty, respectability, age, race, class, gender, or health?
- How does portraiture involve us in spiritual or theological as well as psychological or sociological reflection?

• • •

Let's look at some literary portraits that can teach us a little about portraiture. As you read the passages below, consider what "moves" the writer makes.

- From what angles do we see the subject? At what point in time or space?
- What are the "filters" through which we see?
- How would you identify the writer's tone—their attitude toward the person they're describing?
- How does the writer balance observations with inferences?
- How transparent is the narrator's relationship to the subject?
- Where does the writer use metaphor as a means of characterization? What do the metaphors suggest or invite?
- How long do we linger on a single feature of character?
- How do a character's speech patterns contribute to what we know about them?

Then try writing a close imitation of one of the passages, sentence for sentence, and see what you learn about effective "brushstrokes."

* * *

In this passage from Cherrie Moraga's "La Guera," the author recalls her mother in what appear to be rather conventional terms—birthplace, education, family, marriage, economic situation. But her mother represents a class and perspective on life that offer a sharp contrast to what many still consider middle-class norms, likely different from those of many of her readers. Notice where the passage offers readers challenges or surprises.

> I am the very well-educated daughter of a woman who, by the standards in this country, would be considered largely illiterate. My mother was born in Santa Paula, Southern California, at a time when much of the central valley there was still farm land. Nearly thirty-five years later, in 1948, she was the only daughter of six to marry an anglo, my father.
>
> I remember all of my mother's stories, probably much better than she realizes. She is a fine story-teller, recalling every event of her life with the vividness of the present, noting each detail right down to the cut and color of her dress. I remember stories of her

> being pulled out of school at the ages of five, seven, nine, and eleven to work in the fields, along with her brothers and sisters; stories of her father drinking away whatever small profit she was able to make for the family; of her going the long way home to avoid meeting him on the street, staggering toward the same destination. I remember stories of my mother lying about her age in order to get a job as a hat-check girl at Agua Caliente Racetrack in Tijuana. At fourteen she was the main support of the family. I can still see her walking home alone at 3 a.m., only to turn all her salary and tips over to her mother, who was pregnant again.

Notice how Moraga creates a double frame: we hear about her mother as she is now—a fine storyteller—and as she depicted herself in the stories she told. Try writing a paragraph about someone you know who has told you stories about themselves, including both your observations of who they are now as storytellers and what you have come to know about them from their stories.

* * *

Anne Lamott's portraits, especially her self-portraits, are generally laced with the edgy humor for which she's become widely known and loved. In *Hard Laughter*, one of her earlier books in which her father's brain cancer is a central focus, the humor offers a counterpoint to the very real grief and bewilderment she felt in witnessing the decline of a much-loved and much-admired parent. In this passage the "comic relief" she introduces by describing the family's odd neighbors takes what many may see as an unnecessarily harsh turn. We might consider, reading it, the ways in which she may be not only recording the desperate amusement she needed in the midst of grief but also intentionally making us uncomfortable with our own capacity for ridicule, and inviting us to notice what it is in us that takes shadowy satisfaction in caricature.

> My next-door neighbors live three hundred feet away and raise worms in big wooden boxes in their front yard. The father and

> both children look much like the weird children one ran into occasionally in grammar school—very, very tiny and vaguely Martian. I hide from this family most of the time. They invite me to their yard parties, and I never show up. They drop by the cabin to discuss better ways to raise worms, and I hide in the bathroom while they knock. The ten-year-old daughter, who is outgoing and sort of striking in a tiny weird Martian sort of way, once told me I should brush my hair more. The little boy, who is five years old and looks like Oscar Levant, once put my alley cat in one of the worm boxes. My cat was not amused. The mother is a stunning blond heiress who makes a tremendous effort to be liked and succeeds in offending and alienating almost everyone with whom she comes in contact, except for her husband, who has as much spark and humor as a cattle tick.

Notice how clearly this passage is about the narrator herself, and what her judgments tell us about her. Notice also how much permission she gives herself to name the feelings, judgments, and bad moments she had with these people. Identify the words or phrases that make it funny. Notice where the passage makes you laugh, and perhaps where it makes you uncomfortable. And remember the context: she's grieving, and one dimension of grief is anger.

Try writing a paragraph about people you've found odd, unsettling, or "weird," including moments when you've recoiled or hid or otherwise reacted to their behaviors. Give yourself complete permission to try this; you don't have to publish it, and they don't have to see it, but do also notice the elements of self-portraiture that emerge as you're doing it.

* * *

In *Notes of a Native Son* James Baldwin also focuses on his father in a way that moves from portraiture to self-portraiture. Notice some of the ways it compares and contrasts with Moraga's portrait of her mother.

> I had not known my father very well. We had got on badly, partly because we shared, in our different fashions, the vice of stubborn pride. When he was dead I realized that I had hardly ever spoken to him. When he had been dead a long time I began to wish I had. It seems to be typical of life in America, where opportunities, real and fancied, are thicker than anywhere else on the globe, that the second generation has no time to talk to the first. No one, including my father, seems to have known exactly how old he was, but his mother had been born during slavery. He was of the first generation of free men. He, along with thousands of other Negroes, came North after 1919 and I was part of that generation which had never seen the landscape of what Negroes sometimes call the Old Country.

Notice how the writer moves from his personal difficulties with his father to the social patterns and history that shaped their lives and the forces that separate one generation from the next. Notice the narrative distance he takes on what may have been real emotional challenges.

Try writing a paragraph about someone older with whom your relationship was limited by the very different social or economic or historical circumstances of your lives, contextualizing your and their experience with an observation or two about the broader history of your generations.

* * *

To help your reader discern with compassion and imagination who's there, try these exercises in portraiture.

Write a list, as varied as possible, of "things I've noticed about you/them" with a particular person or persons in mind.

Write short sketches of a person (a few sentences) in terms of . . .

some need or longing or compulsion that drives them
certain habits that define them
their relationship to money
their aging / season of life
their voice and its effect
what they've often said or tend to say in certain circumstances
how they differ from others in their social category
their vulnerabilities: what they seem to hide or protect
their conduct of a particular relationship

Write a couple of sentences in which a gesture or action or posture or facial expression gives a sense of what the subject is experiencing.

Write a few sentences presenting a person in terms of your relationship to them.

* * *

One way to think about the work of writing about other people is that you are "bearing witness" to their lives. "For the dead and the living, we must bear witness," Elie Wiesel writes. For him the dead were the millions who died in concentration camps he survived. They left him with a clear sense of obligation. Historians in recent decades have more frequently and explicitly taken on the task of bearing witness to undocumented lives that have been too often left out of the historical record—the illiterate, the poor, the enslaved, the displaced. Maybe some of these are your people and you can write about them from "inside" or intimate access. Since you have the privilege of literacy, and a desire to write, which is its own calling, consider how you may be called to bear witness. That calling may be situational: you may be the one in a position to tell the story where others aren't. It may be by appointment: others may ask you to tell stories they don't feel equipped to tell.

When you take on the task of writing about someone else in order to bear witness, consider these questions:

- What does it mean in this instance to "bear witness"? How do I honor the truth of this person's life or character and for what particular purpose? To whom do I hope to make it matter?
- What is hard about writing a brief, ordinary account of a life—an obituary, tribute, introduction, or retrospective?
- When is the temptation to sentimentalize or romanticize strongest? How do I hold the distinction between "honoring" and "whitewashing"?
- If I am called to bear witness to someone's criminality or misdeeds, whose interests am I serving?
- If I am the one "in a position to know" and disclose what others may have a right to know, how do I weigh confidentiality against my obligation to them?
- How do I decide in what terms to present someone for others' consideration? In terms of their needs? Their public acts? The effect of their presence? Their gifts? Their lineage? How they fulfill their social roles? The ways they either represent or challenge common notions of "type"?

Consider the above questions as they apply to collective commemoration or recognition—how we speak with or for, say, the "honored dead."

Try this: In a few sentences . . .

Offer a fresh view of a public figure you assume your readers know.

Write about a biblical or historical figure who has served you as a model.
Tell how a person you've known intimately has been faithful to the terms of the life they were given.
Tell about how a person exercises authority.
Offer a word of public praise or indictment.

Or try a longer passage . . .

Develop a scene in which the subject carries out an ordinary task, varying comment on what they're doing and feeling, how they respond to an interruption. Consider writing with a particular adverb in mind: they're doing this work prayerfully, resentfully, absently, with pleasure, wearily, diligently, etc.
Develop a scene in which a subject responds to a public crisis.
Develop a scene in which you recall doing something with the person you're describing, acknowledging your different styles, methods, tensions, rhythms, habits, etc.
Develop a portrait beginning with an epigraph from the Bible or a work of literature.

* * *

Here are a few short examples to play with:

> This book is dedicated to my grandfather and to his habit of keeping books with such marvelously terrifying illustrations down on the bottom shelf where any little kid could read it.
>
> —R. Lee Smith, *The Scholomance*

Try writing a dedication that gets at something you value about a person in a line or two.

> His dad had told him many times that the definition of a real man is one who cries without shame, reads poetry with his heart, feels opera in his soul, and does what's necessary to defend a woman.
>
> —Delia Owens, *Where the Crawdads Sing*

Describe someone in terms of a message you know was formative for them.

> Everything about her spoke of alternatives and possibilities that if considered too deeply would wreak havoc with the neat plan I had laid out for my life.
>
> —Tsitsi Dangarembga, *Nervous Conditions*

Describe a person in terms of the early effect they had on you.

* * *

Portraiture is intimate work. Inevitably it will take you close to boundaries where you have to consider the matter of the subject's right to privacy. And it will involve you in speculation as you try to imagine, and invite readers to imagine, the person's interiority: feelings, motives, fears, hopes, strategies of defense, moments of compassion. As you venture into "the interior," consider these questions:

- What is the value of imagining or speculating on others' inner lives?
- How do you understand the idea of "an intimate portrait"?
- How do we know what we know about others' inner lives? Spirituality? Pain?
- How might personality profile instruments like the Myers-Briggs Type Indicator or the Enneagram help us interpret what we observe in another person's behavior?
- How do we maintain a healthy sense of the difference between empathetic curiosity and voyeurism? What is "holy curiosity"? "Morbid curiosity"?
- How do we decide what's "our business" as we observe and imagine others?

In a few sentences:

- describe a person at prayer, maintaining both respectful distance and intimacy
- describe a person holding a very sick child
- describe a person in grief
- write a short piece considering "What must [he/she/they] have felt when . . ."

Consider what gives a character "depth." How do you understand "depth"?

In a longer passage:

- Write a description of a person in terms of what they "radiate" or their "vibe" or their serenity, unsettledness, intensity, reserve, etc.
- Write a piece entitled "Being [fill in name of someone you know]" aimed at conveying what it must be like to be that person.
- Write a defense aimed at getting readers to soften their judgment of someone.
- Write a passage that lifts up and honors someone who would quite likely be overlooked, ignored, reviled, or dismissed.

...

Here are a few more short passages in which we see a character in terms of their interiority followed by brief exercises to try:

> Being with him made her feel as though her soul had escaped from the narrow confines of her island country into the vast, extravagant spaces of his. He made her feel as though the world belonged to them—as though it lay before them like an opened frog on a dissecting table, begging to be examined.
>
> —Arundhati Roy, *The God of Small Things*

> She is a friend of my mind. She gather me, man. The pieces I am, she gather them and give them back to me in all the right order.
>
> —Toni Morrison, *Beloved*

Try a sentence or two that conveys how one person may feel in the presence of another.

> It was, he knew, their isolation that had made them so vocal. They thrived in the grandeur of their rage. Yet, underneath their masks they were riddled with self-doubt. He could sense the fear behind the clenched jaw.
>
> —Colum McCann, *Apeirogon*

Try a sentence or two about group behavior that gets at what may drive them.

> Rami often felt that there were nine or ten Israelis inside him, fighting. The conflicted one. The shamed one. The enamored one. The bereaved one. The one who marveled at the blimp's invention. The one who knew the blimp was watching. The one watching back. The one who wanted to be watched. The anarchist. The protester. The one sick and tired of all the seeing.
>
> —Colum McCann, *Apeirogon*

Try imitating this, considering a person/character in terms of their internal conflicts.

* * *

Here's a longer passage to explore and play with, a beautiful portrait of "Old Jack" from Wendell Berry's *Memory of Old Jack.* In this description of an old man's awareness, notice shifts of camera angle, pace, what is called to our attention about his attention, what we get to know and how we get to know it.

> Since before sunup Old Jack has been standing at the edge of the hotel porch, gazing out into the empty street of the town of Port William, and now the sun has risen and covered him from head to foot with light. But not yet with warmth, and in spite of his heavy sheepskin coat he has grown cold. He pays that no mind. When he came out and stopped there at the top of the steps, mindful of the way the weight of his body is taking him, he propped it carefully with his cane and, in the way that has lately grown upon him, left it.
>
> From the barn whose vaned cupola was visible over the house roof against the pale sky, Mat Feltner was calling his cows. Old Jack listened with an eagerness that carried him away from himself; for all his consciousness of where he was, he might have been asleep and dreaming. Mat waited, and called again. And then from the quieting of Mat's voice, Old Jack knew that the cows had come near and that Mat could see them moving up deliberative and shadowy out of the mists and the thinning darkness. And then he heard the barn doors slide open.
>
> Except for the crowing now and then of roosters, the little town and its outskirts were quiet. Old Jack's mind was with Mat there in the barn, stirring about the lives of animals. He knew the solitude that Mat had entered at the beginning of every workday since his son was killed in the war. He knew the stiffness and pain that the tobacco cutting had placed in Mat's back and shoulders and hands. He was aware of the deep somnolence of the hayricks in the loft of the barn.

Try writing a passage that similarly invites us to imagine the interior life or thoughts of an old person who doesn't say much anymore. Help us imagine that person in terms of what he or she knows, remembers, enjoys, looks forward to.

* * *

The term *chiaroscuro*, which many of us learned in art history, is useful as we think about portraiture. It means bright-dark and refers to the ways painters work with tonal contrasts to give dimension to figures and spaces. Analogously, we might think about "shadow work," as we sketch characters.

Shadow is a term Jungian analysts use to talk about unconscious or unacknowledged parts of our psyches. The work of Jungian therapy is to bring what is operating in the shadow into the light and integrate it into our conscious awareness and behavior. We often suppress emotions we're afraid of or ashamed of, or sometimes memories that are painful or threatening.

When we write about other people, fictional or nonfictional, it's worth taking into account the fact that all of us are responding to unconscious pressures in ways others may see when we cannot. I think about Regan's disparaging judgment of her father in *King Lear*: "He hath ever but slenderly known himself." Her observation has an element of the tragic in it, especially in light of Socrates's core teaching about how to live well: "Know thyself." What we know as the hero's "tragic flaw" in ancient Greek drama might be recognized as a shadow element of character, usually pride, that, going unacknowledged, brings about his downfall.

As Jung understood it, the "shadow" can contain not only negative but also positive qualities or tendencies we tend not to see, perhaps because of low self-esteem or false humility, or because we have been taught to see them as defects, though they may actually be strengths.

One of the most famous literary representations of the shadow is Mr. Hyde in Robert Louis Stevenson's *The Strange Case of Dr. Jekyll and Mr. Hyde.* In that story—a parable for modern times—the shadow side of Jekyll is so entirely suppressed it becomes a separate self whose life and behavior are in every respect Jekyll's opposite. The story invites us to reflect on what we have individually or collectively suppressed and how it manifests under social or political pressure.

Consider how you might depict a person in the grip of an unaccountable compulsion, and conversely, how you might depict a person who seems to have achieved a "wholeness" of being—integrated the shadow—who is mature in self-knowledge and unafraid—who can say with one of Shakespeare's characters, "The thing of darkness I acknowledge mine."

* * *

All portraiture involves paradox, since we all live among conflicting currents and find ourselves pulled at times in opposite directions. To honor that feature of character, try describing a person in terms of a "virtue" that has become a liability—someone who needs always to be the most generous or giving; someone who is intrusively humble or self-subordinating, relentlessly cheerful, oppressively motherly, overbearingly attentive, nauseatingly "pious," etc. How might that behavior be a response to a fear or need? Consider, as painters do, how you might use light-dark contrasts in the space of a paragraph or scene to make readers aware of the shadow.

Describe a person who's perennially afraid of . . .

being left out
being thought ignorant
losing
being humiliated
being found unattractive
being thought proud or vain
being thought too sexy or unsexy
being in the spotlight

* * *

Try any of these prompts to get at the "shadow" dimension of a character (and consider using them when you write a self-portrait!)

He seemed driven by a need to . . .
She needed to win every argument.
He clearly felt he couldn't afford to . . .
She didn't seem to realize her effect on those around her.
He's always quick to notice . . .
She's always keeping score.
He wondered why no one . . .
She can't let go of . . .
He can't make himself . . .

. . .

Write a bit of dialogue in which a character begins with one of these claims:

I would never be the one to . . .
I can't stand people who . . .
I just don't want to know . . .
I'm addicted to . . .
I need to know . . .

. . .

Before we leave the topic of the shadow, let's talk about collective portraits. Consider what we as a culture/society have refused to look at, denied, repressed, marginalized, ignored, or discounted. *Who manifests the collective shadow?* What do they look like? As you think about that question, you might recall some of these characters or types from familiar stories: witches, Lady Macbeth, Iago (from *Othello*), wicked queens, Hester Prynne, Huck Finn, the Godfather.

Consider also those characters or figures who represent the wisdom of those who have integrated the shadow—who know themselves and acknowledge the fullness of who they are: Kent (in *King*

Lear), Prospero (in *The Tempest*), Lincoln, Gandhi, Gandalf, Ultima (in *Bless Me, Ultima*), Baby Suggs (in *Beloved*). What do you think they mirror back to you individually, or to us as a culture?

* * *

Here, from Joseph Heller's unforgettable satire *Catch-22*, is a brief excerpt from a portrait of a consummate rationalizer—someone who effectively avoids self-confrontation and has made an art of that avoidance:

> It was miraculous. It was almost no trick at all, he saw, to turn vice into virtue and slander into truth, impotence into abstinence, arrogance into humility, plunder into philanthropy, thievery into honor, blasphemy into wisdom, brutality into patriotism, and sadism into justice. Anybody could do it; it required no brains at all. It merely required no character.

Collective rationalizing to promote the agendas of those in power generally goes by the name of propaganda. In these lines from Wilfred Owen's searing war poem "*Dulce et Decorum Est*," the speaker calls out the collective shadow—that part of us that buys into convenient lies or lies we imagine protect our interests over those of others:

> If in some smothering dreams, you too could pace
> Behind the wagon that we flung him in,
> And watch the white eyes writhing in his face,
> His hanging face, like a devil's sick of sin;
> If you could hear, at every jolt, the blood
> Come gargling from the froth-corrupted lungs,
> Obscene as cancer, bitter as the cud
> Of vile, incurable sores on innocent tongues,—
> My friend, you would not tell with such high zest
> To children ardent for some desperate glory,

> The old Lie: *Dulce et decorum est*
> *Pro patria mori.*

Again and again war stories have challenged what Owen calls "the old Lie" and depicted soldiers not as valiant heroes but as victims of a cruel system that turns them into "cannon fodder," dehumanizing them even as "the enemy" are also dehumanized. Consider how you might similarly call out some part of the collective shadow as you think about what we are led to buy into, to normalize, to excuse too readily, to overlook or ignore. As Owen does, you might take aim at a common practice or slogan or ad copy that teaches us to accept the unacceptable, then offer a portrait of those upon whom the collective shadow falls. Instead of soldiers you might focus on shoppers, for instance—consumers who have been conditioned never to think of underpaid sweatshop labor or migrant workers.

* * *

As you reflect on collective portraiture, consider how we still invoke terms like *my people* and *those people*. The idea of "a people" is ancient, of course, and central both to the Bible and the Qur'an: "O my people, they which lead thee cause thee to err, and destroy the way of thy paths," Isaiah writes (3:12 KJV). And in the Qur'an a similar repeated invocation: "O my people, serve God." In both cases, it is God who speaks to identify "my people" as his own. But "my people" readily morphs into a tribal or nationalistic idea when it becomes possessive or defensive or self-referential. And "those people" may be gathered conveniently into a group, all conveniently tarred with the same brush and represented in ways that obscure their individuality.

Once people are consigned to categories and represented as an anonymous crowd, it becomes harder to see them as equal to those we see at closer range as individuals like us with interior lives and mitigating circumstances. "Those people" become at best a backdrop to the more interesting stories and actions of "my people," at worst foils or targets. Creating categories like this is a standard abuse of power—one that becomes unnoticeable the more we passively accept the control device of identifying whole populations for exclusion. Then, as Noam Chomsky warns, power of the few over the many becomes easier to seize and abuse: "The more you can increase fear of . . . welfare mothers, immigrants and aliens," he writes, "the more you control all of the people."

Try this: Jot down some notes for yourself in response to each of the questions below. Use them as an occasion to situate yourself as a writer—a person who speaks publicly and can influence others in the ways they think about particular groups.

Whom do you think you have some right (or duty) to speak for, speak on behalf of, represent? Consider how you might situate yourself to speak about these "others."

Who are the people you think of as "my people"—those you think of, for good or ill, as inhabiting a similar cultural environment, whose assumptions overlap with yours, with whom you identify or socialize, whom you feel comfortable critiquing "from the inside"?

How might you speak purposefully about, for instance, . . .

people of your age (give or take five years)
people of your religious or political persuasion
people who have acquired a skill set similar to yours
people who have suffered in the same way you have (an illness, for instance)

Consider in what terms you might write or speak about any of the following, and what questions you might ask them. (Feel free to pick your own category of people.)

evangelicals
health-care workers
Palestinians
the "über-rich"
teachers
white people
undocumented immigrants
kids in gangs
protestors
police
your grandmother's generation

...

Try imitating or commenting on the brief examples below of passages where writers represent others collectively:

> And I apologize to all of you who are the same age as my grandchildren. And many of you reading this are the same age as my grandchildren. They, like you, are being royally shafted and lied to by our Baby Boomer corporations and government.
>
> —Kurt Vonnegut Jr., *A Man Without a Country*

Notice that Vonnegut names three different groups here, identifying one as victims and two as perpetrators of cultural evils.

> Amal, I believe that most Americans do not love as we do. It is not for any inherent deficiency or superiority in them. They live in the safe, shallow parts that rarely push human emotions into the depths where we dwell.
>
> —Susan Abulhawa, *Mornings in Jenin*

Notice how this characterization is delivered from one character who lives in the Middle East to another, both of whom see Americans as different from themselves. Abulhawa's novel gives American readers a chance to look at themselves from a Middle Easterner's point of view and perhaps be surprised into taking new measure of the degree to which their behaviors, assumptions, and values are culture-bound.

> "Blue-collar workers" have jobs requiring just as much brainpower as "white-collar professionals." To run a family farm is to be a business owner in a complicated industry. But, unlike many jobs requiring smarts and creativity, working a farm summons the body's intelligence, too.
>
> —Sarah Smarsh, *Heartland: A Memoir of Working Hard and Being Broke in the Richest Country on Earth*

Notice how the writer challenges two stereotypes by simple reminding and reframing, in one sentence dissolving the perceived differences between the two groups by redefining farmwork in terms many may not imagine it. Think how you might identify her tone in both the lines quoted and the title.

> The poor have less control than the affluent over their private decisions, less insulation from the cold machinery of government, less agility to navigate around the pitfalls of a frenetic world driven by technology and competition. Their personal mistakes have larger consequences, and their personal achievements yield smaller returns.
>
> —David Shipler, *The Working Poor*

Notice that this list of what the poor have and don't have doesn't mention money. Deftly, the writer identifies what the poor lack or need—control, choice, protection, social recognition—in terms that must give the reader pause.

> Elite networking forums like the Aspen Institute and the Clinton Global Initiative groom the rich to be self-appointed leaders of social change, taking on the problems people like them have been instrumental in creating or sustaining.
>
> —Anand Giridharadas, *Winners Take All*

Notice how the writer imbeds loaded words like *elite*, *groom*, *self-appointed*, and *people like them*. One can read those descriptors and the verb as spin, or as an effort to support his overall argument that what we have normalized—the power the very wealthy exercise over the rest of the population—needs to be recognized as a function of deliberate, systematic manipulation.

> Rather than rely on race, we use our criminal justice system to label people of color "criminals" and then engage in all the practices we supposedly left behind. Today it is perfectly legal to discriminate against criminals in nearly all the ways that it was once legal to discriminate against African Americans. Once you're labeled a felon, the old forms of discrimination—employment discrimination, housing discrimination, denial of the right to vote, denial of educational opportunity, denial of food stamps and other public benefits, and exclusion from jury service—are suddenly legal. . . . We have not ended racial caste in America; we have merely redesigned it.
>
> —Michelle Alexander, *The New Jim Crow*

Notice how the writer foregrounds manipulation of language itself, or labeling, as an essential dimension of an oppressive, expensive, unjust prison system. Consider especially her point that language itself is not simply a neutral tool, but a factor in the ways we understand and address political and social problems—and even what we frame as problems.

* * *

Art history as well as literary history is full of self-portraits. It is, of course, the whole object of autobiography or memoir—presenting oneself in terms that serve particular purposes. Those terms vary, even within a single long narrative. They're generally quite selective. Political autobiography, for instance, might serve the purpose of self-exoneration. Spiritual autobiography might serve the purpose of testifying to divine grace. A biography like *The Education of Henry Adams* serves the purpose of understanding the social forces that have shaped one's values or worldview.

Rebecca Solnit, herself deft at sidelong self-portraiture, writes this about the challenge of self-presentation in *The Faraway Nearby*:

> Listen: you are not yourself, you are crowds of others, you are as leaky a vessel as was ever made, you have spent vast amounts of your life as someone else, as people who died long ago, as people who never lived, as strangers you never met. The usual I we are given has all the tidy containment of the kind of character the realist novel specializes in and none of the porousness of our every waking moment, the loose threads, the strange dreams, the forgettings and misrememberings, the portions of a life lived through others' stories, the incoherence and inconsistency, the pantheon of dei ex machina and the companionability of ghosts. There are other ways of telling.

Her words echo Walt Whitman's famous, expansive claim in *Leaves of Grass*: "I am large, I contain multitudes."

* * *

A self-portrait can be a confession, a correction, a reinventing of self. Self-portraiture can raise new questions about yourself or answer old ones.

Try this: Write a few paragraphs of self-portraiture from any of the following prompts:

When no one is nearby, I . . .
In the quiet I can go inside myself and find . . .
You'll recognize me. I'm the one who . . .
I used to think the one thing that made me different was . . .
If my point is to introduce myself, I'll have to begin with . . .
My story is about healing . . .
Look at me once and you'll see. . . . Look again and you may notice . . .

Adam Zagaziewski's poem "Self-Portrait" offers a delightful example of self-portraiture as a way of reclaiming oneself and one's life by taking stock of it—habits, tastes, preferences, values—making the poem a gesture of self-awareness and self-acceptance. It begins with lines that situate the speaker among the tools of his trade: "Between the computer, a pencil, and a typewriter / half my day passes. One day it will be half a century." Notice how even those lines give us a sketch of a poet's way of being in the world. They make me think of John Donne's line about how a man and his beloved may "make of one small room an everywhere." Because of its length, I don't include the text of Zagaziewski's poem here, but it is readily available at https://poets.org/poem/self-portrait. Look it up, read it through, and try imitating it, either in poetry or in prose, making a longish inventory of what has become of you and some of the ways in which you know yourself.

...

Consider three painters' self-portraits. Noticing how visual artists work and naming what you see in visual art can be a wonderful way to enhance your attentiveness as a reader. As you've seen, I often invoke metaphors from other arts (camera work, framing, melody, drumbeat, brushstrokes, chiaroscuro, etc.) to talk about reading and writing. See how this little exercise may help you as you work with the challenges of literary portraiture. Keep in mind as you look at reproductions of artists' self-portraits (available online at thedraw ingsource.com/self-portrait-drawings.html) the terms in which the artist has invited us to see. Make a list of things you notice about one artist's self-presentation. Include your own speculations.

GET TO KNOW YOUR NARRATOR

You're both the fire and the water that extinguishes it. You're the narrator, the protagonist, and the sidekick. You're the storyteller and the story told. You are somebody's something, but you are also your you.

—*John Green*

"You" aren't the narrator. You may have made up the story in your head. You may even be drawing from personal memories. But you are different from the persona who speaks on the page. Who is telling the story? Who is the speaker in the poem? It's worth getting to know that person.

Even though most of my work is personal nonfiction or poetry, even though I try to write authentically out of lived experience and speak from my heart, in the course of my writing life I have recognized different "voices" not only in retrospect but as I write. At times I've become aware that the person who speaks on the page speaks in her own distinctive tone or cadence or idiom—not far from what I think of as "my own" voice but distinct enough for me to think of her as "her." On a couple of occasions, I actually gave her a name and wrote under a pseudonym—short pieces about sensitive subjects I wanted to speak about in public while also protecting people close to me. Of course, I told the editors I would be writing under a pseudonym. They were fine with it, so I wrote the pieces and discovered a lot about my alter ego, Kate. I'd always wanted to be named Kate. I associated the name with spunky, funny, smart, brave women—Kate in *The Taming of the Shrew*, Kate Hepburn, and more recently Kate Bowler, whose books about living with cancer are lively, edgy, funny, and brave.

My Kate turned out, as I've bemusedly acknowledged to friends, to be smarter, more subversive, and funnier than I am. Writing as Kate allowed me to claim permission I might not have claimed otherwise. I haven't written under a pseudonym since, but doing so a few times taught me something worth learning: I have voices in me that need special permission or invitation to speak. It's good, now and then, to invite them.

Pseudonym or not, whether you're writing fiction, nonfiction, or poetry, your narrator is not your self. You find an angle of vision, a persona, a mood, perhaps a dimension of your own character, and develop that presence as you write. Sometimes your narrator will surprise you. They may be a little quirkier, blunter, more authoritative, or more ambiguous than you are. In this chapter we'll experiment with letting a narrator emerge in ways that might stretch you into a different voice and perspective. You might try speaking as a person far older than yourself, or from another era, or inhabiting a mythic figure. The persona you allow to tell the story or speak the poem you write may take you by surprise. There may be a whole cluster of narrators in your rich, mysterious psyche waiting for a chance to speak. Let them speak and see what they have to say.

* * *

Think of narrators you know. What do you remember about them? How do you remember the voice of David Copperfield, for instance, who assures us that "in great aims and in small, I have always been thoroughly in earnest"? Or the storyteller in the Harry Potter series, or the slow, drawling voice that takes us into *Absalom, Absalom!* with a 123-word sentence? I wrote a small book at one point (*Reading like a Serpent*) about the narrator in *The Scarlet Letter*, who is arguably the main and most interesting character in that deceptively simple story.

Once you've perused your bookshelf, noticing what you notice about narrators, take a look at something you've written. Who's speaking? Who's in there? What do they want? What are they inviting the reader to do? Challenging the reader to get over a prejudice or wait or laugh or empathize? When you "hear" and inhabit that voice, what qualities come with it? Spunkiness? Archness? Conviction? Playfulness? Wit? Gentleness? How do they feel about the events and people they're telling about? How much "air time" does your narrator get relative to other characters—in other words, how much do the characters speak for themselves and how much does the narrator intervene to explain, interpret, correct, or make judgments? What's that narrator not willing to do? to disclose? to concede? About what is that narrator unwilling to take a strong stand? Are they willing to risk readers' judgment? to express ambivalence?

These questions are pertinent not only to fiction or nonfiction in which the narrator is introducing other characters but also to essays or poetry. There's always a speaker. The speaker is always speaking from someplace that is not the whole of who you are and not, after all, "omniscient," though sometimes they might pretend to know it all.

* * *

Try these exercises in narrative positioning.

- Write from a particular role: as a parent; as a friend cautioning or admonishing a close friend about a foolish choice; as a naïve observer at a gathering where you have no expertise; as a concerned parishioner or citizen. Do you like the voice that emerges? Would you listen to this person? Would you readily believe them? Do you detect a note of irony?
- Write three sentences of a letter to someone you believe is abusing power or heedlessly incompetent. Speak from a position of fully justified moral outrage. Do you find that voice moving or persuasive? Do you find yourself egging this voice on or wishing the voice would tone it down?

- Write three sentences delivering alarming news to people whose panic you hope to forestall. Is the voice that delivers that news solemnly prophetic? Panicked? How does the voice communicate a sense of urgency?
- Write three sentences that make it clear you can afford to question or challenge a group you belong to. Write from a place of comfortable authority and authorization. Would you be inclined to trust that person's judgments? To accept the correction? Is it generously offered? Is the authority well established?
- Write three sentences that come from a place of enthusiastic fascination with something many people might think is uninteresting or off-putting (recent research on snail mucus, for example, or what's in the fine print of online consent forms). Are you finding yourself gripped by something you might otherwise have found either boring or disgusting?
- Write three sentences that position you as a voice of reason among extremists. There's a challenge for our time. Is that voice inviting enough to bridge an ideological chasm?
- **Read** like an apprentice: What can you learn about narrators from each of these writers?

Notice with what elaborate ambiguity Nathaniel Hawthorne's narrator in the first chapter of *The Scarlet Letter* describes the prison door through which Hester Prynne, whom we have not yet seen, is about to appear:

> On one side of the portal, and rooted almost at the threshold, was a wild rose-bush, covered, in this month of June, with its delicate gems, which might be imagined to offer their fragrance and fragile beauty to the prisoner as he went in, and to the condemned criminal as he came forth to his doom, in token that the deep heart of Nature could pity and be kind to him.

> This rose-bush, by a strange chance, has been kept alive in history; but whether it had merely survived out of the stern old wilderness, so long after the fall of the gigantic pines and oaks that originally overshadowed it,—or whether, as there is fair authority for believing, it had sprung up under the footsteps of the sainted Ann Hutchinson, as she entered the prison-door,—we shall not take upon us to determine. Finding it so directly on the threshold of our narrative, which is now about to issue from that inauspicious portal, we could hardly do otherwise than pluck one of its flowers, and present it to the reader. It may serve, let us hope, to symbolize some sweet moral blossom, that may be found along the track, or relieve the darkening close of a tale of human frailty and sorrow.

Before you dismiss this leisurely nineteenth-century male voice as mannered and stuffy, consider how he's playing with the very conventions he seems to be observing. More often than not, when he offers an observation he turns right around and questions or undercuts it. You, dear reader, are left to judge, but are deftly reminded you're not really in a position to judge—not just a bit of literary gamesmanship but a rather large moral point—one, you might recall, that Jesus made. To quote briefly from my book on the subject of Hawthorne's narrator:

> This narrator has irritated and confused generations of readers. He gives with one hand and takes with another. He offers judgments, reconsiders, then abdicates altogether with a "be that as it may," or a "so it was said," or a coy observation that it were improper, indelicate, or untimely to arrive at a conclusive assessment of the incidents just recounted. He revels in paradox, inference, and indeterminacy. He keeps tossing us readers the ball, sometimes addressing us directly, standing in indeterminate space and time with one foot outside the frame, at times privy to the most intimate thoughts and feelings of the characters, and at other times abjectly

> dependent upon hearsay and scraps of barely decipherable evidence, like the most abject historian facing the gaps in a partial and dubious record.

> **Try this:** In a paragraph or so, offer a reader observations about a situation you've witnessed, or a public or historical event, making it clear why it matters, and then make it clear why neither you nor your reader is in a position to judge. Be playful about this: be a trickster whose job it is to tell the truth slant to people who might not hear it if it were more directly put. Get around your reader's defenses.

* * *

Here's a very different narrator from Richard Wagamese's *Embers: One Ojibway's Meditations.* Wagamese, a member of a First Nations tribe in Canada, is much respected among contemporary readers. Consider how this narrator makes you feel: how he establishes trust, authority, relationship with the reader.

> Sometimes people just need to talk. They need to be heard. They need the validation of my time, my silence, my unspoken compassion. They don't need advice, sympathy or counselling. They need to hear the sound of their own voices speaking their own truths, articulating their own feelings, as those may be at a particular moment. Then, when they're finished, they simply need a nod of the head, a pat on the shoulder or a hug. I'm learning that sometimes silence really is golden, and that sometimes "Fuck, eh?" is as spiritual a thing as needs to be said.

Wagamese's narrator speaks with an authority the author himself, a member of the Ojibwe tribe, might claim, having weathered an exceptionally difficult childhood and relied on help from strangers at the Children's Aid Society. His narrator here delivers a clear, simple message about what people need, reinforced by repetition: they need . . . they need . . . they need. But then he begins a sentence with "I'm learning," which shifts the focus from his authority to his humility: he's a person who is still in a process of learning or refining what he has come to understand. When the paragraph concludes with the surprising Canadian exclamation, "Fuck, eh?"—a gesture of unpolished camaraderie, we have to laugh, and perhaps modify our developing sense of who, and how, he is.

> **Try this**: Speak as one who knows, but is also learning, what children need, or what struggling artists need, or what arrogant people need, or what people in confusion need. Surprise us, once you've established a tone of voice that conveys both authority and humility, with some expression that makes us laugh—or at least imagine how that voice might sound on a given day, right in the thick of a hard conversation.

* * *

Many of us met Nick Carraway, the narrator of F. Scott Fitzgerald's *The Great Gatsby*, in high school. If our English teachers did their job well, they asked us some questions about Nick, hoping we'd notice the paradoxical combination of innocence and arrogance along with wry humor that gave the whole story a subjectivity we might both identify with and regard with a bit of skepticism. Here's how Nick introduces himself as the story begins:

> In my younger and more vulnerable years my father gave me some advice that I've been turning over in my mind ever since. "Whenever you feel like criticizing anyone," he told me, "just remember that all the people in this world haven't had the advantages that you've had."

> He didn't say any more, but we've always been unusually communicative in a reserved way, and I understood that he meant a great deal more than that. In consequence, I'm inclined to reserve all judgements, a habit that has opened up many curious natures to me and also made me the victim of not a few veteran bores. The abnormal mind is quick to detect and attach itself to this quality when it appears in a normal person, and so it came about that in college I was unjustly accused of being a politician, because I was privy to the secret griefs of wild, unknown men. Most of the confidences were unsought—frequently I have feigned sleep, preoccupation, or a hostile levity when I realized by some unmistakable sign that an intimate revelation was quivering on the horizon; for the intimate revelations of young men, or at least the terms in which they express them, are usually plagiaristic and marred by obvious suppressions. Reserving judgements is a matter of infinite hope. I am still a little afraid of missing something if I forget that, as my father snobbishly suggested, and I snobbishly repeat, a sense of the fundamental decencies is parcelled out unequally at birth.

Notice that even as Nick claims he reserves judgments, he's making them, though he also seems to be aware of his own snobbishness in the final sentence of the paragraph. Notice the confiding tone, the way he seems to invite the reader into a certain friendly intimacy. Notice how, even though he's rather transparently confident in his privilege, and even a bit arrogant, he may, in fact, induce you to trust him, not only by his easy familiarity but because he seems to have given thought to what he thinks of himself and others—seems to be a person capable of both wide observation and self-reflection.

Try this: Noting some of the particular moves of this narrator—his asides, his descriptors, the way he recalls particular incidents—introduce your own narrator, following this pattern: introduce yourself in terms of what you learned when you were younger, perhaps from a parent, that has served you well in particular cases. Tell the kind of circumstances in which it has served you well. And in the course of that, expose some flaw—a slight arrogance, entitlement, self-centeredness, or naïveté, for instance—that the reader might detect even while finding your narrator engaging.

* * *

Colum McCann's *Apeirogon* offers a memorable example of a story narrated in numbered fragments, threaded together by recurrent motifs that come together to give us two fathers' stories of daughters killed in the crossfire of Israeli-Palestinian conflict. The unidentified narrator changes vantage point repeatedly, sometimes seeming to speak from the memory of one of the fathers, sometimes from the point of view of a scholar-historian or a reporter or a bystander. Consider how the narrative voice works in these few fragments.

467

One instant there, the next gone. Whisked out of midair.

466

Water dissolves more substances than any other liquid, even acid.

465

It disrupts the forces of attraction that hold molecules together.

464

In many West Bank houses you fill basins, you line up jugs, you top up bottles by the kitchen sink. You brush your teeth with the tap off. You step quickly from the shower. You put a plastic stopper above the drain in the bathroom. You soak sponges in the standing water. You put aerators on the faucets to reduce the flow. You use a broom to clean the steps, no mops. You wipe your car with a dry cloth. You dust the windows of your house. You know the water can be turned off for weeks at a time and then you will have to buy it at four times the price charged to those across the valley. You climb the stairs to the flat concrete roof and you check the black tanks for leaks. You lift the lid to check the level. You pray for rain even if the tank is almost full.

463

One of the games played by Israeli soldiers is Shoot the Water Tank: the lower the bullet on the tank, the finer the marksman.

462

Sometimes a vindictive Palestinian Authority soldier takes aim too.

Notice even in these short spurts of thought or observation or memory how the level of intimacy, the historical perspective, the frame, the form of address all shift. Notice in all of them, however, an unsettling matter-of-factness about enormities of violence and loss that are a constant throughout the book. The multiplicity of perspectives doesn't allow us to become too entrenched in one point of view, but it does expand our sympathies, as we can see in fragment 464. We are immediately shocked into remembering the ambient hostilities and dangers in 463, just as we have come to a moment of identification with the innocents who live at constant risk. The descending numbers occur in the second half of the book for reasons made clear at the beginning: chapters move from 1 to 500 and then count back down.

Try this: Recall a scene or period in which public events affected private life and see if, in a series of numbered fragments, you can give glimpses from different angles on what happened, how it felt to different parties, what preceded it, either in recent or in ancient history. Experiment with matter-of-factness—few modifiers, little emotive language, letting the facts—the nouns and verbs—evoke the emotional response.

• • •

Finally, in Adam Zagajewski's poem "Try to Praise the Mutilated World" (easily available online) notice how the narrator's address to the reader shifts from encouragement (*Try to praise*) to a stronger tone of admonishment (*You must praise*) to a slightly softened appeal (*You should praise*) and finally to a simple imperative: *Praise the mutilated world.* Notice how the reminders of scenes and memories that follow each support the tonal shift—how the narrator seems to be looking for a way to get the hearer to praise, even though there might well be cause for dismay or even despair. Notice how the urgency grows.

Try this: Either in a poem or in prose, try a sequence of four direct addresses to the reader, imitating the sequence in this poem, adding a sentence after each to support the manner of appeal. See what happens as you feel your narrator's approach shift. See what happens when you end with an imperative and notice what comes to you each time as you change position.

• • •

Experimenting with narrative voice and stance and strategy can teach you a lot about yourself—how comfortable you are with your own authority, or with ambiguity; how flexible you can be about letting the reader make judgments you don't control; how challenging and revealing it can be to destabilize the point of view from which you tell your tale.

ADDRESS YOUR DEAR READERS

Reader, I married him.

—Charlotte Brontë

Good writing is relational. Whether you're writing a letter or a lab report, you're writing to *someone*. There's a person at the other end of the transaction. There's a person at the other end of this one, dear reader. The tradition of direct address to readers, of course, is as old as letters themselves. Letters have specific and known readers, but even they are acts of imagination; the writer has to assume they're catching the reader in a particular state of receptivity or resistance. Open letters, op-eds, or group letters require strategic appeals to whole groups of people whose responses may differ, but all of whom have similar interests at stake.

Letters as such are increasingly rare. Some people manage to write emails that closely resemble the letters people used to handwrite on stationery, but the medium makes them different. I'll spare you my ramblings, sometimes rants, on the value of handwriting and the loss we incur as it atrophies. I will, however, digress long enough to say that, on one of my most memorable trips to the famous Huntington Library in Pasadena, I secured the privilege of sitting at a well-lit table, under the watchful eye of the special collections librarian, reading through a trove of Henry James's handwritten letters. I taught a senior seminar on his novels and felt, as I read his letters, that I was entering intimate spaces in a remarkable life and mind more accessible and moving and deeply human than even his most personable introductions and essays. I continue to be grateful for that encounter.

Open letters, written to particular people but published for others to read as well, can be an effective way of allowing a wide public to enter what seems to be personal or intimate space, at their best preserving both the immediacy and relational character of the letter and the power of a public voice. Of course, they can go awry. They can seem like posturing, or simply a form of pretense. But if you think of the apostle Paul's letters to young churches, or of Rilke's *Letters to a Young Poet*, or of Martin Luther King's "Letter from Birmingham Jail," or of C. S. Lewis's *Letters to Malcolm, Chiefly on Prayer*, or of Bobby Henderson's satirical "Open Letter to the Kansas Schoolboard," or of Eva Tolage's open letter from Tanzania to President Obama, just to mention a few, it becomes clear that open letters occupy an interesting, respectable, lasting place among literary genres and historical documents.

A variant on open letters is the epistolary novel—fiction written in the form of letters—which has its own long, interesting history from the eighteenth-century classics, *Pamela* and *The Sorrows of Young Werther*, to *The Color Purple* to *The Guernsey Literary and Potato Peel Pie Society*. Young adult fiction offers a rich range of these, as well, from Jean Webster's *Daddy Long Legs* to Gaby Dunn's *I Hate Everyone but You*. Now that many kids grow up writing few, if any, actual letters, the genre has acquired a certain quaintness, but also freshness. It allows us to "overhear" a private conversation or a privileged interior monologue.

All writing is an address to the reader. Any writer might say with Emily Dickinson, "This is my letter to the world that never wrote to me." Even if there's no addressee at the top of the page, a writer can adopt a narrative voice that conveys a sense of intense or offhand or conspiratorial personal address, for example. Some, like Robert Browning's "dramatic monologues" or T. S. Eliot's "The Love Song of J. Alfred Prufrock," address a "you" not there—either a putative character who never appears "on stage" or, unsettlingly, the reader as unsuspecting participant in an unfolding plot.

Dedication pages themselves are reminders of private audiences. When we read "For Jenna and James who make it all matter," we are aware that we are witnesses to an intimate act—that the book in our hands is a gift of love or respect first of all to someone who mattered greatly to the writer, and that the rest of us get to enter a space that's already been defined by hope and good intention and love.

An interesting question to ask yourself as you begin to narrate is what you most want from your readers. Trust? Appreciative amusement? Or, if you're Poe, uneasy, half-willing consent to keep moving into darkening chambers? Or if you're Melville, a game willingness to stay the course with someone who calls himself Ishmael, though he may or may not be, and who pretty much assures us of his unreliability at the outset?

* * *

Think for a moment about the relationship you'd most like with your reader. Writing can be relational in a variety of ways. Those I mention here aren't mutually exclusive, but as you look at the examples below, consider which qualities approximate most closely what you aim at—or naturally fall into—when you write.

And consider what experience you want your readers to have. What you write should require something of your readers. Do you want them, for instance, to relax and be entertained and laugh with you? Do you want them to shift nervously in their chairs because they're unsettled or disturbed or feeling a bit of dread? (If you're Poe, this is exactly what you want.) Do you want them to recognize that they were thinking about something too simply? To examine their consciences? To wise up and stop being gullible? To open their closed hearts?

* * *

When you write, you are entering a social contract with your readers—sometimes even a sacred covenant. You are asking them to trust that what you've written is worth anywhere from ten minutes to many hours of their time. You're implicitly promising that it will be worth it: they'll finish the final paragraph feeling or knowing or hoping for something that hadn't occurred to them in that way before.

One way to keep yourself conscious of your social—or sacred—contract with your readers is now and then to invoke the "dear reader" tradition. Look up a few instances of it and try it out. Addressing the reader directly (*Dear Reader, . . .*) makes a bridge from the impersonal page to the person sitting in a recliner holding the book. It's a reminder that the one who speaks is aware of the one who listens, and cares about them enough to offer them this gift.

Imagine those readers. Are they the kind who need to be convinced the story is worth their time? Are they hungry for the information or hope or reassurance you offer? Are they allies? Adversaries? Novices? Peers? Of course you don't know. You may have readers who fall into all those categories. Still, it can be helpful to imagine them, not only their attitudes but the situations in which they might be reading your work. The context in which you write and the context in which your readers read both matter. Your place in the real world, and theirs, shape the transaction.

* * *

Let's see how a few writers have appealed to their "dear readers."

Charlotte Brontë's impassioned aside to readers in *Jane Eyre* offers some memorable moments of human contact that seem to reach across space and time to affirm our fellowship in suffering:

> Gentle reader, may you never feel what I then felt! May your eyes never shed such stormy, scalding, heart-wrung tears as poured from mine. May you never appeal to Heaven in prayers so hopeless and so agonised as in that hour left my lips: for never may you, like me, dread to be the instrument of evil to what you wholly love.

This famous, heart-wrenching epistolary moment has carried a blessing from Charlotte Brontë to generations of readers. Her Jane wishes us well. She hopes we will be spared what she suffered. She also sweetly imagines that we, too, would dread to be "instruments of evil" to those we love—and in assuming that, she offers a bit of moral instruction: We should all hope to avoid doing harm to those given to us to love. The intimacy of this wish, so urgently expressed, aligns our moral sensibilities with Jane's for a moment as she generously assumes the best of us.

It is only a moment. This address to the reader works in the same way as a theatrical "aside" where the actor turns from his dialogue with another character to address the audience directly—impart a secret, share a plan, render a wry judgment. Then, like the actor on stage, Jane returns to telling her story. But we're a little closer in now. Feeling cared about, we care about her a little more and a little differently. We feel her vulnerability and her sorrow and her dread and her loss. As a young reader might put it, "We're all in"—allies now, or protectors, or sympathetic friends.

* * *

A generation before Brontë, E. T. A. Hoffmann endeared himself to a wide audience of German readers by sidling up to them similarly. In *The Golden Pot and Other Tales*, for instance, his narrator poses the reader a direct, and perhaps uncomfortable, question about their experience of discouragement or despair:

> Let me ask you outright, gentle reader, if there have not been hours, indeed whole days and weeks of your life, during which all your usual activities were painfully repugnant, and everything you believed in and valued seemed foolish and worthless?

Are you not like me? in other words. Don't we all fall into melancholy or desolation or even cynicism? Had Hoffmann left off the opening phrase, "Let me ask you outright, gentle reader," and simply posed the rhetorical question, the effect would have been quite different. Certainly, we wouldn't give it quite such earnest personal consideration as he invites here. But because he pauses to turn and look us in the eye, as it were, we pause, too, and reflect at least for the space of a paragraph on our own dark moments. Notice, too, how he prolongs the query with little repetitions or intensifiers: "hours, indeed whole days and weeks"; "usual activities," and more than that, "everything you believed in and valued"; "foolish and worthless." There's nothing in the question that doesn't seem to this narrator to bear repeating as he leans into the space between us to emphasize how urgently he wants us to remember.

* * *

Fyodor Dostoyevsky, writing *White Nights* in 1848, comfortably acquainted with the tradition of authorial intrusion, addresses his readers as his contemporaries—people who have achieved a similar maturity and are capable of retrospection and the poignant self-awareness that comes with age: "It was a wonderful night, such a night as is only possible when we are young, dear reader." A couple of decades later, in *Notes from Underground*, he gives us a narrator much less inclined to be companionable: "No," he explains, defending himself from those he presumes to be his antagonists, "I refuse to consult a doctor from spite. That you probably will not understand. Well, I understand it, though." We are thrust into the role not only of antagonists, but of dull and unsympathetic ones. It's a curious and daring gambit, but one that serves purposes that unfold slowly and painfully in the course of a psychodrama not unlike many of Poe's. We venture forward almost on a dare. Jarring experiments like these serve to remind us—dear readers who are reading as writers looking for strategies to steal—that we can cast our readers in whatever roles we want to offer them: fellow travelers, objects of pity, confidants, colleagues or collaborators, the uninitiated waiting for instruction, or the faithful waiting for a word of blessing.

Only two decades later, Mark Twain puts a characteristic ironic spin on this technique in *The Innocents Abroad* when he alludes to the reader in the third person—an affectation that in some times and places indicated particular respect, though in Twain's hands it comes with wry irony and perhaps a sidelong grin:

> The gentle reader will never, never know what a consummate ass he can become until he goes abroad. I speak now, of course, in the supposition that the gentle reader has not been abroad, and therefore is not already a consummate ass. If the case be otherwise, I beg his pardon and extend to him the cordial hand of fellowship and call him brother. I shall always delight to meet an ass after my own heart when I have finished my travels.

This edgy invitation to recognize humbly that few of us are truly cosmopolitan, that until we cross cultural boundaries, we're likely to remain unaware of our own prejudices and blinders, amounts, in the course of this humorously self-critical narrative, to a critique of nationalism and insularity.

Twain's very different contemporary, Henry James, accomplished similar authorial intrusions somewhat more subtly by occasionally speaking in the first person in a narrative that might otherwise seem comfortably "omniscient." Because they are so rare in James's copious novels, little flags like "I give this little sketch . . ." or "As I have said . . ." can bring us up short and reintroduce the disturbing question whether we are indeed hearing an impartial case. As a student once put it, James's narrator suddenly jumps out from behind a tree. We'd forgotten he was there.

In more recent fiction partiality is much more readily accepted as a norm: we've learned in the course of our reading lives (not to mention our political lives) that all narrators are unreliable. What's interesting about them is the way in which they're unreliable. Perhaps we can't rely on them for historical accuracy, but we can rely on them to surprise us into seeing something we hadn't thought of in just that way before. Perhaps we can rely on them to challenge gender stereotypes but can't rely on them to do justice to the historical contexts of what they criticize. And so on. Consider your own reliability. What are you most eager to convey? What are you willing, if not eager, to elide or suppress? How do you understand writerly integrity?

Try this: As an exercise in focus, write out a two-sentence contract with your reader that names what they have a right to expect of you, and the claim you feel authorized to make on them: "*Dear Reader, as you pick this up, you have a right to expect that I will. . . . I, in turn, expect that, if you want to get the full value of what I have to offer here, you will. . . .*" I'm not recommending inserting this into your current manuscript, but it may serve to clarify your own purposes in ways that help you hear your own voice as you read over your story.

Contemporary writers keep playing with the "Dear Reader" tradition in new ways. Its slightly antique, quaint effect (salutations of any kind are increasingly omitted in electronic communication) lends itself to good-natured parody or playful imitation of the kind Judith Martin popularized in her wry tome on etiquette, *Miss Manners*. To a letter written presumably from a discontented young person, she replies cryptically, "GENTLE READER, Growing up is the best revenge." Shonda Rhimes, a hugely successful TV writer and producer, adopts the device in her memoir, *Year of Yes*, as a full-frontal self-introduction: "Gentle reader, may you never be lucky. I am not lucky. You know what I am? I am smart, I am talented, I take advantage of the opportunities that come my way and I work really, really hard." And Marie Brennan, in *A Natural History of Dragons*, uses it to surprise readers into awareness that they are participants in constructing the fictions they're engaging, responsible for all the technical effects they may bring with them from long experience with commercial film: "If you wish, gentle reader, you may augment your mental tableau with dramatic orchestral accompaniment."

Direct address to the reader may serve simply to frame a narrative in which no further authorial intrusion occurs. Kate DiCamillo, in *The Tale of Despereaux*, opens with it to give the ensuing story the effect of something told—perhaps on a dark night in the semisecrecy of a closed circle:

> The world is dark, and light is precious.
> Come closer, dear reader.
> You must trust me.
> I am telling you a story.

"You must trust me" has the interesting effect of reminding the reader that narrators are inherently limited and not entirely trustworthy—that suspending disbelief, entering a story on the writer's terms, is an act of trust not yet wholly justified by evidence.

At the opposite end of a narrative, an authorial intrusion can be used to send the reader back out into the world with a little blessing—a hope that they might take something from their journey through the story that will equip them for that world. In *Once upon a River* Diane Setterfield offers this gentle leave taking:

> And now, dear reader, the story is over. It is time for you to cross the bridge once more and return to the world you came from. This river, which is and is not the Thames, must continue flowing without you. You have haunted here long enough, and besides, you surely have rivers of your own to attend to?

More surprising in its intimacy, Rick Riordan, popular author of fiction for young adults, takes a similar opportunity in closing *The*

Tower of Nero to step outside the narrative frame and reminds the reader that they are fellow inhabitants of the real world:

> So, dear reader, we have come to the end of my trials. You have followed me through five volumes of adventures and six months of pain and suffering. By my reckoning, you have read two hundred and ten of my haiku. Like Meg, you surely deserve a reward. What would you accept? I am fresh out of unicorns. However, anytime you take aim and prepare to fire your best shot, anytime you seek to put your emotions into a song or poem, know that I am smiling on you. We are friends now. Call on me. I will be there for you.

I don't know that anyone has called Rick Riordan in response to that invitation. But I'd guess at least one reader may have taken him up on the offer, forgetting that there's always a chasm that separates narrator from author like the one that separates the portrait from the face. Those who address us from the pages of a book are mere images or shadows "till," as C. S. Lewis put it, "we have faces."

WRITE FROM INSIDE OUT

"The weight of this sad time we must obey;
speak what we feel, not what we ought to say."

—William Shakespeare

I realized I had been navigating a slippery gray area when one of my advisors observed, handing back the final draft of my dissertation, "It doesn't look exactly like a dissertation. I'm not sure what I'd call it, but I like it." I'm not entirely sure she meant it as a compliment. At the time, most dissertations, even in literature and the arts, were written in a distinctly academic style—impersonal, authoritative presentations of the results of research. The "I" who wrote seldom appeared on the page.

I went back to graduate school after almost a decade of doing other important things. I loved returning to learning. It was consoling in a hard time. I loved reading and writing again, loved discovering new ways to read. There was nothing impersonal about any of it. So when I set out to write about the autobiographical writing of people who had been through shattering life crises, I wrote very much in the first person. My own curiosities, my sympathies, my noticings, and, along with those, my admiration for the courage of those writers were very much a part of the research experience. What piqued my deeply personal interest in their literary experiments as acts of healing was part of what I wrote about.

With whatever reservations they may have harbored about its informality, my committee granted me the degree, for which I'm grateful. More importantly, though, I learned from that sustained period of writing something about how to write that I've never forgotten: write from inside out. Be faithful to the curiosity or the longing or the urgency that got you started. Find out what you find out and talk about the process along the way. Not everything you write is, or should be, memoir. But everything you write has your heartbeat in it—the you that wonders, feels, is taken by surprise, is disappointed, has to reconsider or deal with ambiguities and the you who wants to share what you're finding out. So write from that place. As I said in the previous chapter, all writing is relational.

This chapter is an invitation to experiment with different kinds of personal writing and the different voices we mentioned earlier that speak within you as you write. In that sense it may apply primarily to memoir, but memoir overlaps, as all genres do, with any kind of writing that leads you into personal exploration, self-reflective musing, moments of revelation and surprise you couldn't have planned. What you're writing may not have started out as memoir but might at some point start to look suspiciously like it. It's also an invitation to try being unabashedly subjective: find what gives you pleasure in the process of telling anything you have to tell. Share that pleasure with your reader.

Remember—when you're writing from or about your own experience, you can shape your material any way you like. You can be selective. You can tell the good parts. You can leave out what you decide doesn't matter or isn't any of your reader's business. As you write, you'll be finding a balance between what's special or even unique about your story and what's representative about it—how your story, fiction or nonfiction or the moments you share in lyrical poems, testifies to something true about living in a particular class, region, or generation.

* * *

Let's say you're working with your own life material, either in a memoir, or in poems, or in a series of personal essays. **Consider these things:**

Consider alternatives to chronology. You don't have to travel along a timeline. You can organize your story by theme or by relationship or around particular kinds of events—learning moments, surprises, significant encounters.

Consider what stories and archetypes have shaped you, provided models, defined your ideas of hope, courage, heroism, evil, etc. How, for instance, does your approach to what you have to tell involve a narrative of overcoming obstacles or shouldering responsibility or being given a second chance, or proving people in your position have a claim to authority?

Consider your purposes: life writing can be . . .

a legacy
a warning
a corrective or protest
an offering of love
a path to intimacy
a strategy of advocacy
an act of self-defense
an experiment
an act of radical reconstruction
an inventory
a way of letting go
a way of keeping
a confession/disclosure
a comedy
a testimony of faith

Consider your audience. For example . . .

those who love you and whose lives are linked to yours
those who think they've known you but haven't known the half of it
those who suffer from similar conditions, anxieties, losses to yours
those who have something practical to learn from your story

Start with moments, vignettes. Go where memory or inclination or inspiration leads you and tell about particular incidents. Reorganization can come later. And remember the following:

You have more than one story to tell, and more than one way to tell it. Think of the archetypes again: you can write as victim, as survivor, as explorer, as curious outsider, as snarky critic, as sympathetic fellow traveler, as naïve observer.

You can afford to play, digress, experiment, reframe. You can tell the same scene twice in two different ways, making the point that you see it differently now, or that memory is not always reliable, always mingled with imagination, edited according to taste and capable of revision.

You don't have to "get through" anything. You can linger. Your story may have a trajectory you can trace—or more than one—but the goal posts aren't stationary. Writing it changes it; in the course of arranging incidents, moments may move into the foreground or recede into the background and your sense of purpose itself may shift.

Your story can take any form:

first-person memoir or autobiography
a series of poems
a collection of vignettes, each of which opens up its own reflection on some dimension of loss, recovery, reengagement, spiritual wrestling and growth, etc.

a reconstructed journal (possibly with present-time commentary)
a series of short, reflective essays
a series of interviews in which someone else poses the questions

Your story will involve others' stories. Consider how to tell them. You might write a multivoiced narrative, for instance, that includes your story, your mother's story, your father's story, a sibling's story, and shorter chapters by various caregivers and friends.

* * *

Let's take a look at how a few writers have established personal relationship with readers by writing from inside out. Notice how we become acquainted with Mary Rose O'Reilley, for instance, in her delightful personal narrative, *The Barn at the End of the World: The Apprenticeship of a Quaker Buddhist Shepherd*:

> Thirty years ago, I was hanging out one night in London, wearing a black trench coat and smoking an unfiltered Gauloise—working, that is, on some more-than-usually-obnoxious false persona—when a woman approached me with her two teenaged children and began to chat. They told me they were Quakers, and in some mysterious way they attracted me so powerfully, despite the pretentious image I was cultivating at the time, that I wanted to *baah!* like a sheep and follow them home. Why? I don't know. I wanted to get into the soft light that held those people. So I understand how Jesus could say to someone, "Follow me," and they'd drop everything. Indeed, dropping everything is half the fun.

Each of the excerpts below is introduced by a question to consider. As you read, notice closely the writer's choices—what details, what verbs and verb tenses, what use of time and space, what distance is taken on the scene presented. Consider again what you can learn from these writers about the difference a small stylistic choice might make. What can you learn about what you find enlivening, inviting, off-putting, or unsettling?

* * *

In these excerpts from Maya Angelou's autobiography, *I Know Why the Caged Bird Sings*, consider how the present, adult "I" presents the past, child "I." What enables you to imagine the relationship between them? How the adult feels about the child? What she most wants us to understand about (1) the child and (2) the adult who represents her?

> Without willing it, I had gone from being ignorant of being ignorant to being aware of being aware. And the worst part of my awareness was that I didn't know what I was aware of. I knew I knew very little, but I was certain that the things I had yet to learn wouldn't be taught to me at George Washington High School.

> If growing up is painful for the Southern Black girl, being aware of her displacement is the rust on the razor that threatens the throat. It is an unnecessary insult.

> As I ate she began the first of what we later called "my lessons in living." She said that I must always be intolerant of ignorance but understanding of illiteracy. That some people, unable to go to school, were more educated and even more intelligent than college professors. She encouraged me to listen carefully to what country people called mother wit. That in those homely sayings was couched the collective wisdom of generations.

* * *

In the following brief excerpts from Maxine Hong Kingston's autobiography *The Woman Warrior*, consider how her use of the present tense serves to conflate present and past experiences—to present the past experience as if felt with equal immediacy in the present. Or consider how the details she provides about her mother also provide information about herself and her points of view, past and present.

> Nobody supports me at the expense of his own adventure. Then I get bitter: I am not loved enough to be supported. That I am not a burden has to compensate for the sad envy when I look at women loved enough to be supported. Even now China wraps double binds around my feet.
>
> My mother has told me once and for all the useful parts. She will add nothing unless powered by necessity, a riverbank that guides her life. She plants vegetable gardens rather than lawns; she carries the odd-shaped tomatoes home from the field and eats food left for the gods.

> In America my mother has eyes as strong as boulders, never once skittering off a face, but she has not learned to place decorations and phonograph needles, nor has she stopped seeing land on the other side of the oceans. Now her eyes include the relatives in China, as they once included my father smiling and smiling in his many western outfits, a different one for each photograph that he sent from America.

* * *

In the following short excerpts from Joy Harjo's writings, poetry and prose, consider how she challenges the reader to think about the very experience of self-awareness.

> My father told me that some voices are so true they can be used as weapons, can maneuver the weather, change time. He said that a voice that powerful can walk away from the singer if it is shamed.

After my father left us, I learned that some voices can deceive you. There is a top layer and there is a bottom, and they don't match.

I could hear my abandoned dreams making a racket in my soul.

I sit up in the dark drenched in longing. / I am carrying over a thousand names for blue that I didn't have at dusk.

I wanted to see everything. It was around the time I acquired language, or even before that time, when something happened that changed my relationship to the spin of the world. My concept of language, of what was possible with music was changed by this revelatory moment. It changed even the way I look at the sun.

. . . My father staggering in drunk, beating my mother, the shame and hate in him burning, burning. Then he'd hit my brothers. And then me whom it was said he loved most. He'd save me for last, when his anger was ashes, when the fire was hottest. And then he'd hold me, "Sugar, sugar," he'd croon, the tears so thick they made a lake on the linoleum floor.

* * *

In the following brief excerpts from Ta-Nehisi Coates's *Between the World and Me*, consider again the relationship between present and past self, and how the writer situates the reader: What are you invited or challenged to do?

So I feared not just the violence of this world but the rules designed to protect you from it, the rules that would have you contort your body to address the block, and contort again to be taken seriously by colleagues, and contort again so as not to give the police a reason. All my life I'd heard people tell their black boys and black girls to "be twice as good," which is to say "accept half as much." These words would be spoken with a veneer of religious nobility, as though they evidenced some unspoken quality, some undetected courage, when in fact all they evidenced was the gun to our head and the hand in our pocket. This is how we lose our softness. This is how they steal our right to smile.

The pursuit of knowing was freedom to me, the right to declare your own curiosities and follow them through all manner of books. I was made for the library, not the classroom. The classroom was a jail of other people's interests. The library was open, unending, free. Slowly, I was discovering myself.

I was learning the craft of poetry, which really was an intensive version of what my mother had taught me all those years ago—the craft of writing as the art of thinking. Poetry aims for an economy of truth—loose and useless words must be discarded, and I found that these loose and useless words were not separate from loose and useless thoughts.

* * *

In the following short excerpts from Kathleen Norris, *Dakota: A Spiritual Geography*, consider how what the speaker sees defines her, invites the reader to consider inner landscape in terms of outer landscape, and reveals something about "self" by refraction:

For me, walking in a hard Dakota wind can be like staring at the ocean: humbled before its immensity, I also have a sense of being at home on this planet, my blood so like the sea in chemical composition, my every cell partaking of air. I live about as far from the sea as is possible in North America, yet I walk in a turbulent ocean. Maybe that child was right when he told me that the world is upside-down here, and this is where angels drown.

I was in my early forties the first time I visited an oncology ward for terminal patients. I was apprehensive, as I was going to the front lines of a battle our culture labors mightily to keep hidden, but I needed to visit a friend. I did not expect that the ward would be an apocalypse in the literal sense of the word—an unmasking or uncovering. The intensity of misery was overwhelming, yet it did not frighten or repel me, for I had entered holy ground. People my own age, as well as the elderly, were shockingly frail and needed support just to totter down the hall. Still, they were alive, and walking, saying their goodbyes to friends, children, and grandchildren. What struck me was that the atmosphere was not merely one of sadness, but also one of beauty deepened by the sobering inevitability of death, and blessed by the presence of vibrant love. While the relentless activity of New York City surrounded us, here everything unessential had been stripped away. Only life remained, a gift and a joy beyond our understanding. I had arrived in the real world.

Once, when I was describing to a friend from Syracuse, New York, a place on the plains that I love, a ridge above a glacial moraine with a view of almost fifty miles, she asked, "But what is there to see?" The answer, of course, is nothing. Land, sky, and the ever-changing light.

* * *

Here are some approaches to a life story that might start off as lists:

What happened to me
What happened because of me
What I'm able to see that you can't
What you may not understand about me
How I've changed and why
What organizes my daily life, my sense of myself
What I believe in and how that shapes my daily life
What I've had to resist or overcome or cope with
What I know about
Forgiveness, fear, love, jealousy, loss, humor, problem solving, etc.
Why look at the hard things
What I hope for
What one thing I would change if I could
What I save and why
What I've learned to let go
Paintings, books, movies, music that have mattered to me

* * *

As you write, **consider some of these questions**:

Whose life is it, anyway? Try out these ways of addressing that question and see which seems truest to your own understanding of yourself. Which would you want to communicate as you find the voice that speaks to readers you hope for?

You are not your own; you were bought with a price . . .
No man is an island, entire unto himself . . .
We're all in it together . . .
Your life is your assignment . . .
We are stewards of our bodies, our time, our relationships, our gifts

In what sense is "my" story "mine" to tell?

I have a unique point of view
Only I have experienced the particular pains, pleasures, losses, and learnings that belong to my story
No one else is going to do it, or able to do it justice

What truths have I come to that need or deserve to be told?

Which parts of my story will serve me as clarification, confession, or instruments of self-understanding?
Which parts of my story will serve others by offering lessons, examples, historical perspective, a sense of connection with ancestors or the "communion of saints"?
If I decide to omit some parts of my story, what process of discernment has led to that decision, and how might that, also, be useful?

What might it mean to be "bold" in telling my story? Where might timidity be a temptation to resist?

In what ways, if I am to tell the truth, should I be willing to disillusion, displease, or disappoint possible readers of my story?

In what ways might my story offer surprises to those who know me? How might those surprises be helpful?

How might incidents in my life serve as . . .

parables?
sources of amusement?
sources of encouragement?
sources of practical instruction?

How do I tell about suffering without self-pity?

about achievements without undue pride?
about failures without crippling regret?
about difficult relationships without blame?

In what ways might my story serve either to affirm something important or to challenge or protest something objectionable?

* * *

Try these exercises in retrospection:

Detail a particular scene as thoroughly as possible. How many visual details, smells, sounds, words, interruptions, feelings can you retrieve with what you think to be reasonable accuracy? Where are you aware of verging into imagination to fill in gaps?

Write about how a particular scene, either in memory or story, has served as a reference point, a parable, a learning moment in your life? How has it served you in that way since it occurred?

Consider the complexity of a particular scene or season in your life. See how precisely you can name the ambivalences, uncertainties, complicating factors, conflicted feelings.

Consider just one dimension of your life and growth and trace that growth in no more than ten incidents or "steps" or inflection points. (I learned this particular way of getting into life material at a workshop with Ira Progoff, a student of Jung.) For instance, trace . . .

the life of your body
your spiritual development
your progress in understanding and managing money
your growing awareness of contexts of action, systems we live in, forces at work
your deepening commitment to a particular cause
your growth in understanding a key relationship
your struggle with a particular weakness or lack

Write a list of questions to yourself and answer them. For example:

What helped shape my political sympathies?
What habits do I still carry from my family of origin?
Where do I lay blame, and what would happen if I lifted that blame?
What have I managed to reframe? What might I still need to reframe in order to understand it more complexly or compassionately?
What does it mean to me to take full responsibility?

Also consider:

What difference has it made?
Why has it stayed in conscious memory?
What has it come to symbolize or represent?
How do you measure the distance between then and now?

Here are some kinds of moments to recall:

a moment when you learned something about yourself, or another
a moment of intellectual or spiritual awakening
a moment when you let something go
a moment of complete contentment
a moment of sadness
an encounter that gave you new confidence
a moment of rage
a moment of laughing at yourself
a moment when you were "surprised by joy"
an ordinary moment on an ordinary day

a moment characterized by color or sound
a moment when you said yes to something new
a moment of seeing
a moment when you "lost yourself" in the moment

Consider how the life of your body has provided you with a particular range of possibilities, challenges, limitations, adjustments. Consider, for example:

injuries, wounds, losses
illnesses, chronic and acute
stature, structure, physical gifts
gender, ethnicity, particular standards of beauty

Consider when you have been particularly grateful for your body; or frustrated with it; or when you have particularly enjoyed living in it.

Consider the role of particular physical senses in how you have developed relationships with God, self, others, the natural world:

taste
touch
vision
hearing
smell

Recount particular moments when each of these has provided you with a moment of discovery, heightened awareness, epiphany. Consider the particular adaptations and acceptances that have been a necessary and important part of the "assignment" to live in and through your body. How has aging brought new awareness and new decisions?

Consider the activities that have contributed to your "bodily intelligence." What, for instance, have you learned from tennis or hiking or swimming that has deepened your trust in your body, your sense of confidence, balance, focus, etc.?

Consider the messages you got about bodies as a child, and what you may have had to overcome or resist or revise as you grew older. What inhibitions were transmitted? What notions of gender-appropriate behavior? Modesty? Strength?

How has the life of the body been involved in your spiritual development?

* * *

Public events intrude on our lives, sometimes quite profoundly. Where were you on 9/11? What were the following weeks like for you as the immediate aftermath unfolded?

How did you react on the occasion of a major natural disaster you lived through, witnessed, or read about?

From whom did you hear war stories? How did they shape your sense of war?

Consider the forms of media you have used over the course of your life. How have you adapted?

* * *

Here are a few more life lists to try:

Privileges I've enjoyed
Conflicts I've resolved
Objects I've cherished
Skills I'd like to keep developing
What I've learned to laugh about
What I've learned about how to help
What I depend on
Secret satisfactions of aging
Words of wisdom that have mattered to me
What I've learned to do about difficult people
What I know about money
What I've learned to let go of
Books that have mattered to me
Changes to which I've adapted
What I hope for the children whose elder I am / will be
Important places
What travel has taught me

PLAY ALONG

The noun of self becomes a verb.
This flashpoint of creation in the present moment
is where work and play merge.

—Stephen Nachmanovitch

Stephen Nachmanovitch is a jazz musician deeply interested in what enables people to improvise—invent in the moment, respond to whatever the moment presents. In his book *Free Play: The Power of Improvisation in Life and Art*, he explores the answer to that question by reaching into several spiritual traditions, drawing examples of creative practices from all the arts, and considering how much improvisation may be required of any of us in the course of an ordinary day. Reading it helped me recognize playfulness as a mark of being spiritually awake. People who are playful trust what's given on the spur of the moment and go with it. The first rule in improvisational theater is "Whatever is happening, say yes." Work with it. See what comes up.

While that advice may get you started, it doesn't obviate the need to work out the implications of what you've started. But it does send you into that work awake, refreshed, trusting, smiling, and watchful for what else might come up along the way.

Most practicing artists and writers invoke the language of play in describing their work: An idea came and I played with it. I saw where the scene is going and played it out. I'm playing with possibilities.

It may be easier to see how paint or clay invite play, but words, too, invite play. Many of them mean two things, or sound like each other, or just make you smile, like *quiddity* or *frabjous joy*. Even when you're writing about something you take completely seriously, you can afford to play, and in fact it's healthier for both you and your readers if you do play a little here and there. If you tend to be dead serious (such a sad way of putting it) about your writing, here are some ways to make it more playful work.

* * *

You can play with the sounds and rhythms of words, dropping a bit of iambic pentameter into a line of prose, for instance, or suddenly alliterating or writing a single paragraph that works like a couplet at the end of a sonnet. Or you can actually write a couplet at the end of a sonnet that takes a surprising turn. Shakespeare did that a lot.

Imagine these lines at the end of a tense scene between two characters: "I'm done with this argument," she said, shoving back her chair. "I think I'll go and write myself a poem." A reader might not pick up the iambic pentameter in her last sentence, but someone might, and it's fun to slip it in there. Fun is good.

* * *

You can make nouns into verbs. One of my professors found this practice irritating. He was a product of upper-crusty East Coast training. When I occasionally did make nouns into verbs, he attributed them to the unfortunate deficiencies of my having been educated in the West Coast outback where the rules of grammar had somehow suffered from a history of Western lawlessness. I ceased afflicting him with my noun-verbs. And I agree that too-frequent slippage of this kind would start to look affected or silly. But once in a while it's a playful—and sometimes poetic—way of reminding yourself and your reader that anything can be made into a verb, since (as I believe) everything is a verb. As poet Christian Wiman put it, "Think of the atoms inside a stone." They (and we) are all in constant movement. Playing with grammatical categories can surprise people into thinking large thoughts. You might ponder the verbness of things on your next walk. In the meantime, consider writing a line here and there that breaches grammatical categories for the fun of it:

> She sweatered her way through the winter, longing for the sleevelessness of spring.

or

> I wanted to orange the whole garden, speckling the grass and the clapboards with nasturtiums and marigolds and tiny bright berries and trees with finches.

or

> He wanted to quarterback so badly. Somehow, I couldn't interest him in mastering chess.

or

> We travel well together: she bookstores her way through cities while I museum to my heart's content.

Just remember, if you do this sort of thing too often, you might come off (as a friend of mine Britishly puts it) as "too clever by half."

* * *

Playfulness is more about the spirit you bring to the process than about special effects. One of the best ways to get into writing when your muse has taken a long break and you find yourself lagging is to play with prompts. Sometimes a prompt provides just the little nudge we need to get started, or to pick up and keep going. Prompts are a way of tricking ourselves into writing and seeing what happens without overthinking or overplanning. They're a way of sidestepping *ideas* and leaving room for hunches, sudden impulses, surprises from somewhere other than the superego or the ego-overseer. The best prompts, I think, aren't questions or whole statements to respond to but words, phrases, half sentences that leave a wide-open space to leap into.

* * *

Half sentences give you a little momentum in a particular direction without predetermining where you'll land:

> *Left alone with my thoughts, I naturally reverted to . . .*
> *The look she gave me was hard to describe. It was as though . . .*
> *None of this mattered to me quite as much as . . .*
> *It's hardly an excuse, but . . .*
> *It's a complicated matter, but to put it simply, . . .*
> *This sounds ridiculous, but . . .*

A half-sentence prompt is a little like pushing a kid on a new bike just enough to give them some momentum. Then they're off. You can usually get a whole paragraph out of one prompt before you have to stop and strategize.

* * *

Epigraphs and short passages open up play space. What someone else has written can provide a frame or a teaser or trigger a memory, a character description, or a reflection on an issue or problem. Try writing a few sentences in response to one of these:

> People want you to want what they want. If you want the same things they want, then their want is validated. If you don't want

the same things, your lack of wanting can, to certain people, come across as judgment.

—Ann Patchett, *These Precious Days*

No one is more ingenious than the poor, wherever you find them. When you are poor every stage has to be thought through. Wealth is the opposite. With wealth you get to be thoughtless.

—Zadie Smith, *Swing Time*

I gave him everything from my lunches I hate, which is called Charity.

—David James Duncan, *The Brothers K*

* * *

Writing dialogue is inherently playful. As soon as you write a few lines of conversation, you have voices that imply characters and situation and tensions. If you're stuck on a scene, try writing the conversation first, then see where and how it came about. Use any of these prompts as the first of several lines of dialogue. Or start yourself off with something your mother or third-grade teacher or supervisor might have said.

Absolutely not!
You're thinking of doing what??
I'm baffled.
Can't you find a way to come?
When will you find out?

* * *

Questions can be prompts. If they're open-ended enough, questions put you in dialogue with yourself, which is an entertaining place to be: hearing more than one voice from the internal "committee" (as a friend of mine once helpfully put it) automatically involves you in considering more than one point of view. Questions can help you jump tracks if you're stuck on one and it seems to be leading nowhere. If you're not sure how to develop a thought, try posing a generic question like one of those below and then take a few sentences to answer it. Then you're off and running. (Or if you're not, ask another one.)

Why would that be?
Who would have known?
What might they have done about it?
What if it actually began ten years earlier?
How do I know?
When did it change?
Who knew?
Where were they likely to go?

* * *

Loaded words are prompts, sometimes sharp-edged. Sometimes, as we saw above, a single word has such a charge all you need is to put it on the page and it will energize a response. "Loaded" words are supercharged with the weight of current controversy or historical disrepute or personal associations. These are words you can't drop into a conversation without awakening some kind of felt response. See what comes when you use one of these loaded words as a starter.

plastics
Israel
pipeline
nationalism

Bible
insurance
predator
saint
empire

...

Names can be prompts. Do a little deliberate name-dropping. If you drop a known name into a paragraph, you get a backstory that lends its own color to the story you're telling. Alluding to any of these is likely to add a dimension to what you're telling your reader (I list them deliberately in no particular order):

Moses
Napoleon
Beyoncé
Rachel Maddow
The Virgin Mary
Rosa Parks
Romeo
Sitting Bull
Che Guevara
Gandhi
Jeff Bezos
Taylor Swift
Netanyahu

...

Images can be prompts. Take a long look at something in your field of vision—a tree outside the window where leaves are falling, for instance. Let it be a prompt. Make a simple observation about it: "A leaf just fell" or "The man's head is turned away" or "More than half the painting is sky." See what wants to come next. See if it intersects with what you were writing in the first place, or if it opens a path to a new piece.

Example: *Shakespeare's Sonnet 73 comes to mind more often these days as autumn leaves fall, and as I watch grandchildren move toward maturity and feel warning flashes of pain in stiff knees . . .*

Or look at an image of a person wearing a hat and begin a reflection on it with a simple observation: *I don't wear hats. I own some . . .*

Or look at an image of a raven and let it evoke a memory: *When I was fifteen I memorized half of Poe's "The Raven." . . .*

Prompts are a way to retrieve a spirit of playfulness. Writing can be a struggle; it's not all delight and playfulness and surprise. But as Germaine Greer once said, and I often have reason to recall, "The struggle which is not joyous is the wrong struggle."

• • •

Finally, consider what you might learn from imitating, or at least closely noticing, what's playful in a few passages by writers who have in common the playfulness they bring even to serious subjects. Take careful note of your own responses and exactly what awakens them.

• • •

Sarah Vowell is both an avid amateur historian and a playful—often wryly playful—writer. As in the passage below, she frequently uses an ordinary moment to make a wild leap into observations about historical events, reminding us how closely we are connected to, and implicated in or complicit in, events we might prefer to think of as remote history.

> Just the other day, I was in my neighborhood Starbucks, waiting for the post office to open. I was enjoying a chocolatey cafe mocha when it occurred to me that to drink a mocha is to gulp down the entire history of the New World. From the Spanish exportation of Aztec cacao, and the Dutch invention of the chemical process for making cocoa, on down to the capitalist empire of Hershey, PA, and the lifestyle marketing of Seattle's Starbucks, the modern mocha is a bittersweet concoction of imperialism, genocide, invention, and consumerism served with whipped cream on top.

Try this: Start with a product you regularly use and see if you can trace its history in a few sentences that deepen your own and others' awareness of process. Do it in a way that preserves a sense of curiosity and lively interest rather than judgment or self-judgment.

* * *

Elaine Hsieh Chou in *Disorientation* offers a playful three-sentence description of a place whose miscellaneous details invite us to imagine, with some amusement, worn couches, cheap coffee, and a cat who has a history:

> Though it was a little shabby and could do with more frequent dusting, students flocked to the café for the worn-in armchairs and couches, free wi-fi and cheap coffee. Ingrid particularly liked the topsy-turvy lamps, the bookshelves open for browsing and a live-in cat, Agatha. She was a temperamental, sticky-furred tuxedo who had once single-handedly thwarted an armed robbery.

Try this: Write a few sentences of miscellany that convey slightly comic dishevelment in a place. Include a living being like the cat.

...

In *Dear Girls: Intimate Tales, Untold Secrets & Advice for Living Your Best Life*, Ali Wong adopts the device of a letter to her daughters to deliver often comic, sometimes sharp-edged observations about life in America as nonwhite children of Asian families. Notice how, like Sarah Vowell, she breaks categorical boundaries to unsettle readers first into laughter and then into troubling awareness:

> Then again, if our relatives had been able to Yelp America before coming over, they might have thought twice. Those reviews would have been mixed: "The opportunity is on point, but they kind of overdo it with the institutional racism and the guns. 3 stars."

Try this: Anachronisms are often fun and funny: imagine ancestors doing something very contemporary like posting a Yelp review or sending texts and superimpose our time onto theirs in a way that makes you laugh.

...

Consider how Carole Satyamurti's poem "I Shall Paint My Nails Red" plays with a simple list (notice how many roads lead back to lists!) to skip from one level of motivation to another with a wry, agile self-awareness that invites the reader to consider their own apparently trivial choices. I quote the first few lines; the list continues, and is easily available online. Each line, even the more amusing ones, opens a door to reflection one might have walked past.

I SHALL PAINT MY NAILS RED

Because a bit of colour is a public service.

. . . .

Because it will remind me I'm a woman.
Because I will look like a survivor.
Because I can admire them in traffic jams. . . .

Try this: Compose a "why" list like this, making the reasons / excuses / imagined effects as varied in tone as they are here. See which of the lines might provide a point of departure for a reflective essay.

Not all playfulness is humor, but healthy, life-giving humor requires playfulness. You don't have to be a self-proclaimed humorist to activate your sense of humor as you write, just as you don't have to be a watercolorist to call readers' attention to shades of green in the forest or a musician to allude to the odd, dissonant musicality of urban sounds. There are plenty of ways to give yourself and your readers permission to laugh, or at least smile or lift an eyebrow, even in pieces that are not primarily intended to be funny. Consider some of the varieties of humor: It can be amusing, surprising, hilarious, subtle, edgy, ironic, offhand, impish, incisive, broad, bawdy, clean, hospitable, dark. Lists of types of humor are easy to find online, but it may be helpful to name some of them here as you think about the varieties of playfulness and humor that can be awakened in good writing. Here's a short list:

Satire, which uses the faults of others as constructive social criticism.

Self-deprecating humor, which makes you vulnerable but closer to readers.

Situational humor, based on mundane situations that surprise us into laughter.

Understatement, where you deliberately trivialize; for example, a nuclear war would ruin our vacation plans. Disproportion is the key.

Overstatement, where you make a big deal out of a rather trivial situation.

Gallows humor, which is about something that's painful, hard, or horrifying—well done, it can be a redemptive reminder that we can still afford to laugh.

Hospitable, effective humor takes care, self-awareness, and forethought. Think about your own sense of humor and ask yourself: What kind of humor do I appreciate? What "lines" am I careful not to cross? When have I found myself stifling my laughter because it's "inappropriate"? When do I have to give myself permission to laugh? When have I considered who "has a right" to laugh? When does respect require that some of us refrain from laughing until we're given permission?

A key to finding what's funny is honesty. Simply paying attention to what makes you laugh or smile seems to me more valuable than trying to follow any rules about how to be either playful or humorous in your writing. We all know how painful it can be to see someone trying to be funny and not quite hitting the mark. Better to play it straight if that's truer to your experience of what you're writing about. Still, comedy writers have identified a number of simple techniques that fairly reliably awaken laughter. One is the "rule of three," in which the third item in a series is incongruously related or disproportionate to the first two. Three of anything creates a natural arc—a developing pattern and expectation, as in "I came, I saw, I conquered" or "in thunder, lightning, or in rain." When the third term is either disproportionate or dissimilar, we laugh, for instance, "in thunder, lightning, or in traffic jams." Laughter comes in a moment of recognition—pattern recognition, recognition that possibilities are far wider than our expectations tend to allow.

Another common technique is putting a spin on clichés, again a playful reminder that springs us out of the grooves of patterned behavior and makes us suddenly aware of both the fragility and the malleability of the habits of mind that organize the world. For example, Walter Winchell, in a review of a Broadway show, once famously asked, "Who am I to stone the first cast?" And comedian Jack Handey advised, "Before you criticize someone, walk a mile in their shoes. That way you'll be a mile from them, and you'll have their shoes."

The point here isn't to inventory comic techniques, though those are fun to look up and try. The point is to find and honor your own spirit of playfulness—what makes you laugh—and share it.

Each of these short examples offers something to learn from and play with. Try a bit of imitation and see what comes.

FROM ANNE LAMOTT:

"You can safely assume you've created God in your own image when it turns out that God hates all the same people you do."

Try it: *For a long time I managed to read my own abridged Bible. It left out . . .*

"Not forgiving is like drinking rat poison and then waiting for the rat to die."

Try it: *Deciding you don't need to pray is like . . .*

"I thought such awful thoughts that I cannot even say them out loud because they would make Jesus want to drink gin straight out of the cat dish."

Try it: *I carried around such a long list of resentments I couldn't share them because they would . . .*

"My mind is a neighborhood I try not to go into alone."

Try it: *The thoughts that keep me awake after I turn out the light . . .*

* * *

FROM T. S. ELIOT (OF ALL PEOPLE),
SPEAKING OF A STATE OF HEIGHTENED SPIRITUAL AWARENESS:

The moments of happiness—not the sense of well-being,
fruition, fulfilment, security or affection,
or even a very good dinner, but the sudden illumination . . .

Try a phrase or sentence with a list that ends with a slight incongruity.

Madame Sosostris, famous clairvoyante,
Had a bad cold, nevertheless
Is known to be the wisest woman in Europe,
With a wicked pack of cards.

Try a bit of character portrayal that both elevates and makes comic the same person.

* * *

Brian Doyle, a much beloved writer whose playfulness is well worth learning from, had fun in, among other places, his titles and tables of contents. Consider this list of titles of actual prayers: they show us something about the way playfulness and piety can not only coexist but inform one another.

FROM THE TABLE OF CONTENTS OF *THE BOOK OF UNCOMMON PRAYER*:

- Prayer for Cashiers and Checkout-Counter Folks
- Prayer in Thanks for Decent Shoes
- Prayer of Thanks for All Birds, Herons in Particular
- Prayer for the Men & Women Who Huddle Inside Vast Rain Slickers All Day Holding Up STOP Signs at Construction Sites & Never Appear to Shriek in Despair & Exhaustion
- Prayer for Opossums, You Poor Ugly Disdained Perfect Creatures
- Prayer for Women Named Ethel and Men Named Elmer, for We Will Not See Their Likes Again
- Prayer of Thanks for Good Bishops, as Opposed to Meatheads Who Think They Are Important
- Prayer for My Man Daniel Age Three Who Will Die from Cancer in About Two Weeks
- Prayer of Gratitude & Awe for the Lanky Silent Genius Informational Technology Guy Who Just Fixed My Computer by Glaring at It & Waving His Hand
- Prayer of Awed Thanks for Nurses
- Prayer for the Commonwealth of Australia
- Prayer of Gratitude That There Are Newts in This World
- Prayer of Thanks for the Man or Woman or Child Who Invented Socks
- Quiet Prayer for Friends Whose Teenage Child Just Stormed Out of the House
- Prayer for Cats

- Prayer of Gratitude for Small Things Done Very Well That You Only Notice When You Sit Still & Pay Attention

Here's how one of the prayers begins. See what these few lines show you about playfulness:

> Prayer for Cashiers and Checkout-Counter Folks Who endure the cold swirls of winter from the sliding doors that are opening and closing every forty seconds; and who endure pomposity and buffoonery and minor madness in their customers; and who gently help the shuffling old lady in the ancient camel coat count out the right change for her loaf of bread and single sad can of cat food; and cheerfully also disburse stamps and cash along with bagging the groceries and even occasionally carting them out swiftly for the customers they know are frail and wobbly; . . . And so: amen.

Try a brief imitation—a real prayer of thanks that also invites appreciative amusement.

* * *

One generous, life-giving message you deliver to readers by being playful as you write, allowing surprises to happen, sharing your own moments of quirkiness, is that even in a world where "ignorant armies clash by night," we can afford to be amused.

TELL THE PUBLIC PART

I would not have you descend into your own dream.
I would have you be a conscious citizen of this
terrible and beautiful world.

—*Ta-Nehisi Coates*

I heard about President Kennedy's assassination from my fourth-period history teacher. He was called out of class by someone from the office and returned a minute later with a look on his face I've never forgotten. "The president has been shot," he said. "We're waiting for more information. If you want to leave now and go home, you're free to do so." No one moved. He walked to his desk, put his face in his hands, and began to weep. He was an ex-Marine.

It was a moment of shared bewilderment, shock, uncertainty, and we needed to be with a grown-up who knew what to do. But he didn't. No one did, just then. The people in Washington, DC, knew how to orchestrate a state funeral. But all weekend, as footage of the event itself and the aftermath replaced the usual TV programming, grief and shock were laced with bewilderment. Where—and when—are we now? What just changed in an instant for the generation now living? The question kept unfolding into new answers. That assassination remains an inflection point in my coming of age.

One dimension of any story you have to tell, fictional or nonfictional, is the public or historical context in which it takes place. All of us have lived through or been acutely aware of major public events that shaped us in some way and became touchstones in our coming of age. Biographies, even of people who did not live their lives in the public eye, tend to place life stories in historical contexts that add a dimension of meaning: all lives are subject to both natural and social forces that give them shape. Think of defining public events in your lifetime: it doesn't take much of a stretch to see how your own responses or those of the people around you became personally significant. Consider how any of the following might be a part of the story you have to tell about your own life or about a character belonging to your generation:

- a national election
- a natural catastrophe—earthquake, tsunami, wildfire
- an assassination or death of a public figure
- a piece of landmark legislation
- a pandemic
- a war
- a large economic shift

* * *

Every public event we know about is also personal. Just knowing about it affects us—our sense of danger or safety, our sense of what is normal or predictable, our understanding of how things happen, our hopes. Repercussions always follow. The "butterfly effect" happens. These days we don't have to connect too many dots to see how what happens in Sudan or India or Gaza or Kyiv may be pertinent to our lives and stories, wherever we are on this fragile earth.

So it makes sense somewhere in any story, play, or poem to acknowledge what's happening outside the immediate moment—now and then to widen the social-historical-political frame of reference. Sometimes these acknowledgments are simply time markers: when Toni Morrison opens her searing novel *The Bluest Eye* with the bemusing sentence, "Quiet as its kept, there were no marigolds in the fall of 1941," she leaves us with a number of questions, but also with an awareness that in 1941 war was raging in Europe and the United States was considering whether to enter that war. What ensues isn't a novel about wartime as such, but the date gives us a broad backdrop, a point of reference, and perhaps some implicit metaphors and ironies to consider as the story unfolds.

...

Sometimes a simple allusion is enough to change the tone or perspective of a whole piece. Sylvia Plath's reference to "my skin / Bright as a Nazi lampshade" elicits horrifying images of atrocities that cast a long, dark shadow over the rest of the poem, identifying the speaker in some ways with the victims of those atrocities. The name of the ship in *Moby-Dick*, *Pequod*, alludes to the indigenous Pequot tribe that was defeated in a disastrous war with English colonizers in 1636–1638—one of many threads that connect that epic tale with specific events in American history. A passing reference to "the Crash" in a dialogue between Atticus and Jem in *To Kill a Mockingbird* makes it clear that the Great Depression is a vivid memory for the adults in the novel—a fact that offers some insight into the social pressures and fears that motivate some of them.

...

Public events could figure in your story in other ways:

- where I (or my character) was when it happened
- how I (or he or she) understood it then / understand it now
- what shifted for me (or them) as stories of those most affected emerged
- how it has offered some measure of subsequent events
- how it marked a "before" and "after"

As you find places to broaden your piece to include public events, you might want to consider how you or your character might respond to questions like these:

- What can I not avoid coming to terms with because I live in this particular historical moment?
- When have I had to think about my public identity—generation, race, class, gender, faith community, regional identity, etc.?
- When have I decided to "go public" in the sense of publicly declaring my relationship to a group or event or party or faith?
- What might I include in an essay or chapter called "I'm a Participant" or "I'm Part of This" or "We're in This Together"?
- How might I consider my proximity to a public event a calling—a divine invitation?

* * *

Whatever you're writing—memoir, story, play, poem—the following exercises might help you notice connections between public and private events in your own life or in the story you're telling—how they intersect, change your perceptions of what's happening, move you toward more complex understanding or deeper compassion:

Start with a list:

The first public events I became aware of as a child
Times I realized I had to make a public choice
Events that changed my mind
My public role models
How/when my sense of history shifted

Or try some sentence starters:

Life wasn't the same for anyone after . . .
I've had to consider what I'm willing to know about . . .
Reading/listening to the news, I realize . . .

In a generation and a culture where faith communities are deeply divided, I . . .
From where I stand . . .

• • •

Let's consider what we can learn from writers who connect private and public stories.

John Steinbeck's *The Grapes of Wrath* is an epic story of a family caught up in the Dust Bowl migration and in the social forces at work in a deeply disrupted ecology and economy during the Great Depression. Since the public story is so explicit in this novel, the action of individual characters can always be seen partly as a response to those forces, but not only that. Steinbeck works at the riparian edge where psychology meets political life, allowing us to see, as the ancient Greeks did, how tragedy is always both profoundly personal and widely public in its sources and implications as it invites us to recognize the great cycles of history. Consider how, in this brief passage, the personal and the public or political intersect:

> "Sure," cried the tenant men, "but it's our land. . . . We were born on it, and we got killed on it, died on it. Even if it's no good, it's still ours. . . . That's what makes ownership, not a paper with numbers on it."
>
> "We're sorry. It's not us. It's the monster. The bank isn't like a man."
>
> "Yes, but the bank is only made of men."
>
> "No, you're wrong there—quite wrong there. The bank is something else than men. It happens that every man in a bank hates what the bank does, and yet the bank does it. The bank is something more than men, I tell you. It's the monster. Men made it, but they can't control it."

This bit of dialogue opens a wide door for reflection on philosophy, economics, and human history. It echoes themes we may recognize from Shelley's *Frankenstein* or from Charlie Chaplin's poignant film, *Modern Times*, where he gets caught in a machine trying to keep up with a conveyor belt. For twenty-first-century readers, it points prophetically to the question that still drives controversy over *Citizens United*: Is a corporation a person under the law? What happens when corporations are given the same rights as people?

The genius of stating the problem in a few lines of dialogue is that the men on both sides are caught in the same apparently inexorable forces, unable to control them, and all of them find themselves bewildered by the question of ownership: Does the earth belong to those who inhabit and work on it, or can ownership and profit be completely separated from sweat and labor? The larger question that arises over the power of a "paper with numbers on it" echoes a lineage of argument over natural law. "Where is it written?" is a question that competes with the notion that "possession is nine-tenths of the law." The American history of struggle between indigenous tribes who understood territory as a matter of habitation and belonging and European invaders who claimed land by the power of laws, declarations, and exchanges of money is a long one, and the tragedy of that struggle informs this conversation in a way that gives it scope well beyond the space it occupies on the page.

Notice a few of the "brushstrokes" that make this little exchange effective. One is repetition of the terms *bank* and *monster* in close proximity. Monstrosity in myth and story suggests some form of growth that has exceeded human control and ceased to serve humane purposes. Another key word, though it occurs only once here, is *good*. "Even though it's no good, it's still ours." We have to pause over it to consider what is "good." What are the goods we seek in the pursuit of happiness?

Try this: Write a short scene in which two characters are talking about a public event that is affecting both of them.

* * *

We see a very different example of developing character and scene against a broad public backdrop in R. F. Delderfield's novel *To Serve Them All My Days.* As it begins, a young Welsh veteran of World War I, emerging from treatment for shell shock, hesitantly seeks employment at a rural English school, feeling unsteady, unqualified, and outclassed. In his interview with the kindly headmaster near the beginning of the story, the horrors of that war are introduced frankly and naturally in dialogue. Here the headmaster is answering the young man's misgivings about being able to navigate the post-war world he's returned to, not to mention the class and nationality differences that separate him from the students:

> It's not a matter of years, but of experience, don't you see? What are our casualties to date? Not far short of three million, I'd say, and a third of them dead at eighteen-plus. No one who hasn't been out can imagine what it's like. Mentally a man like you must have aged about a year every month, and that makes you immeasurably senior to theorists like me, and faithful old buffers like Cordwainer, Acton and Gibbs.
>
> Someone has to tackle the job of nudging all those young rascals over the threshold into what I sincerely hope will be an entirely new world.
>
> We can't do it because we're even more adrift than they are and haven't a compass reading between us. In a year or so I dare-say we can find you some help. Hang it all, everyone in his early twenties can't be dead or maimed or gassed. In the meantime you're on your own, lad.

Notice how a gruesome national statistic enlarges our awareness of what the main character has been through. By putting the information into a dialogue between the old headmaster and the young applicant, the author helps us see their generational difference in sharp new terms. In fact, 6 percent of British adult males died in

World War I. To remember that is to have to imagine the young man in the story in terms of shocking, traumatic loss. Part of his character development lies in his frustration at the impossibility of adequately enabling those around him to imagine what he has been through—a recurrent theme in stories of people returning from war. The headmaster at least has some imagination for the young man's psychological isolation when he says, "Mentally a man like you must have aged about a year every month." An observation like that conveys a great deal in a few words about the scope of his compassionate imagination and invites readers to take the historical moment into account in any consideration of this character.

> **Try this**: Consider any of the international or national conflicts in recent years and write a short scene, perhaps a dialogue, in which its personal effect is addressed.

* * *

Ilya Kaminsky's poem "We Lived Happily During the War" (in *Deaf Republic*, available at poetryfoundation.org) offers another striking example of writing into a particular historical moment. It recalls, as the poet acknowledges, his awareness of the 1990 war in Transnistria as the Soviet Union fell apart. We don't need to know that bit of background, however, to recognize how the poem addresses any of us whose awareness of the world includes daily updates about war and brutalities happening elsewhere. With those updates comes awareness of the painfully ironic distance between our own relative comfort and those of people in war zones—not to mention chronic anxiety about when hostilities might become much more local. Reading it, the question "Who is my neighbor" becomes more fraught. Since the poem itself doesn't specify which war is referenced, we may read it with reference to whatever war occupies our thoughts at the time of reading. For some older readers "the war" may still evoke images of World War II—a war few now personally remember, though many of us have seen searing documentary footage and more than a few movies about it. For others the phrase will evoke images of Vietnam or Iraq or Afghanistan or Gaza.

The poem begins with a simple confession, "We lived happily during the war," and goes on to contrast the "we" who lived happily with those whose homes were bombed or whose poverty made them especially vulnerable. It opens with a confession: "And when they bombed other people's houses, we / protested / but not enough, we opposed them, but not / enough." It goes on to locate the speaker as one who lives, not altogether at ease, in "the country of / money, / our great country of money" and toward the end inserts a simple "(forgive us)" before the final reiteration that we "lived happily during the war." The parenthetical "forgive us" puts the reader in the position of confessor and also leaves us to consider: Are we in a position to forgive or might we rather be confessing along with the speaker?

That direct address involves the reader in a new and disturbing way. The poem's uneven lines suggest jagged breathing as we are called into what may be a painful moment of guilty self-awareness. It challenges us to reflect on how we benefit, at least in the short term, from the insularity afforded by money and privilege. It invites us to think concentrically about what is going on "around" us, which may also be going on within us.

One critic, Leah Asmelash of CNN, has said this poem "indicts American passivity toward violence both at home and abroad." The repetition of "not enough" includes in that indictment the many who challenge public atrocities only to the point of salving their own consciences. Imagine a similar poem or passage in which you mention "the war" or "the mass shooting" or "the drought" or "the floods" as a reference point, letting that allusion ironize or frame the scene you're telling.

Try this: Write a poem or passage that puts you (or a character) at the site or moment of a public event and serves to tell us something about character or circumstance by how you/they respond to it. It could simply be emergency vehicles stopping on the street outside, or what's happening on television as two people are having a conversation. Or it could be what happens to one person as many others are either celebrating or panicking or mourning. As you write, consider . . .

ambiguities, tensions, uncertainties
first thoughts and second thoughts
how one might respond to fear or emergency or surprise
what tonal variations you might experiment with

...

Even if you leave the public part mostly implicit, remember that behind everything you write hangs a wide, complicated backdrop—behind the action and time frames of the story and also behind you as you write. Look for ways to acknowledge those as you go.

TELL HOW IT HAPPENED

The work of the historian is not the work of the critic or of the moralist; it is the work of the sleuth and the storyteller, the philosopher and the scientist, the keeper of tales, the sayer of sooth, the teller of truth.

—Jill Lepore

When I was teaching Gabriel Garcia Marquez's *One Hundred Years of Solitude*, a "magical realist" novel in which supernatural or paranormal events occur rather routinely, I asked students how they might attempt to account for it if someone standing in the room suddenly began to levitate. One said she'd assume he was a saint. One said he'd think it was a trick. After a few other conjectures, one student shrugged and said, "I don't know—stuff happens." It seemed like a dodge, but was also an honest answer: There are, as Hamlet put it to Horatio, more things in heaven and earth than are dreamt of in our philosophies. Things happen. We don't always know why.

Happening comes from the term *hap*—"chance." A whole philosophy is imbedded in that bit of etymology. American mainstream culture teaches causality in mostly rationalistic ways. Since the Enlightenment, many in our culture—even people of faith—are less inclined than in earlier centuries to acknowledge the role of mystery, chance, or divine intervention. One of the most interesting dimensions of narrative—factual or fictional—is the way it accounts for how things happened. One thing led to another. A great wind came from the east. By pure coincidence, or by synchronous convergence, or by divine providence, a life-changing moment came about. It happened "in the fullness of time."

In lyric poetry, too, one image or feeling or moment connects to another, often subjectively and surprisingly, in ways that lead us to rethink how those connections occur. In this chapter we'll explore a range of notions about how things happen, and how we may line them up suggestively or surprisingly or sequentially, depending on our purposes. Narrative is a way of making sense of how things occur. Narrative theory is the study of the ways events are shaped into stories. A lot of other people have written books about narrative theory. This is not one. But anyone who writes needs to muse about how things happen and how to account for those happenings.

* * *

Let's move into that question by considering a few writers' thoughts on cause and effect. Lamenting what he saw as Americans' cultural shortcomings, David Foster Wallace, author of *Infinite Jest*, wrote, "All I'm saying is that it's shortsighted to blame TV. It's simply another symptom. TV didn't invent our aesthetic childishness here any more than the Manhattan Project invented aggression." Similarly, both Naomi Klein and Chris Hedges made the point that Donald Trump's rise to power was "a symptom, not a cause." They raise the interesting question of how often we mistake an effect for a cause (and how often we fall into a logical fallacy called *post hoc ergo propter hoc*—after a thing, therefore because of the thing) and invite us to dig a little deeper to establish what happened.

Steven Levitt, coauthor of *Freakonomics*, identified another common flaw in the way we often represent causes and effects:

> We have evolved with a tendency to link causality to things we can touch or feel, not to some distant or difficult phenomenon. We believe especially in near-term causes: a snake bites your friend, he screams with pain, and he dies. The

> snakebite, you conclude, must have killed him. Most of the time, such a reckoning is correct. But when it comes to cause and effect, there is often a trap in such open-and-shut thinking. We smirk now when we think of ancient cultures that embraced faulty causes—the warriors who believed, for instance, that it was their raping of a virgin that brought them victory on the battlefield. But we too embrace faulty causes, usually at the urging of an expert proclaiming a truth in which he has a vested interest.

That's a lot to think about next time you introduce a "because" clause. Most of us aren't going to begin our stories with the big bang or principles of genetics or subatomic physics, but we might find ways to acknowledge the subtlety and mystery of how "chains" of events are related. (The metaphor itself implies a theory.) It's good to bear in mind a claim many have made along with Johnny Rich in *The Human Script*: "The only simple truth is that there is nothing simple in this complex universe. Everything relates. Everything connects."

* * *

Think about how often any of us is asked, "How did it happen?" Or think of how a doctor might ask, "When did it start?" Immediately we search for a point of origin and begin the process of connecting dots that, like clusters of stars in the sky, might be organized into any number of constellations. My parents' story of how they met and married usually began with a crush in fifth grade. Sometimes, though, it began twenty years later when Dad tracked down Mom's family, learned she was in India, and wrote her a letter. It didn't begin, though it could have, with a lonely, displaced kid with a difficult father who found the warmth and kindness he needed in a classroom. It could be a story of destiny or grace or what Caroline Myss calls a "sacred contract" sealed before birth.

Tracing clear lines of cause and effect is vitally important for physicists, engineers, insurance adjusters, and attorneys. When we construct narratives or poetic sequences, it's good to remember that every effect has multiple causes and that we can't trace all of them. Those who tell stories, fictional or nonfictional, make choices about how far back and how widely to trace lines of cause and effect, and when to recognize an action as a reaction. William Faulkner's novels offer a particularly interesting treatment of causality: now and then a paragraph begins with "Because . . . ," even though what came before the because clause appears to be missing. We seem to have dropped into a long conversation midsentence and are conspicuously reminded that we're being invited in as latecomers—very like life.

Psychologist Carl Jung wrote extensively about "synchronicity," which he called an "acausal connecting principle." It refers to a simultaneous occurrence of events that appear to be meaningfully related but have no apparent causal connection. What most of us call coincidence often opens a door to mystery: not every convergence can be explained. Or maybe you're one who leans, as I do, toward the view that there are no coincidences. There's grace. Or providence. Or fate. Or destiny. Or forces too subtle to notice or name are at work like "the force that through the green fuse drives the flower."

* * *

As an exercise in ways of accounting for how things happen, **try writing a simple narrative** (or a simple list) detailing one of these.

How you ended up living where you do
How a project idea came about
How you arrived at a life-changing decision
How an accident happened
What made you change your mind
Or, if you're ambitious, how history led us to this watershed political moment

As you think (and tell) about how these things happen, consider how you might address any of the following questions:

What forces were at work?
What were the circumstantial or confluent factors?
Who was behind the scenes?
Do I believe "there are no coincidences"?
What was afoot?
What was God up to here?

As you continue your reflection on causes, consider verbs that offer images of process. Ask any of the above questions about some current event in your life and see what shifts if you postpone assigning agency:

What's emerging?
What's unfolding?
What's erupting?
What's shifting?
In what new direction are things tending?
What's diminishing?
What's opening up? Closing down?
What's softening? Drying up?
What's repeating itself?
What's revealing itself in new ways?
What's looming?
What's gathering?

* * *

I've always maintained that one of the main purposes of an education is to be able to look at anything and think about process: Take a look at any concrete object in your field of vision and consider the story (all the activity—all the verbs) behind it.

Where was it mined/harvested/manufactured? Who designed it; who paid them; who was at the workbench; who protected their rights; who packaged it, marketed it, transported it, decided what space it would occupy? If you haven't seen it, visit the website for the project called "The Story of Stuff": https://www.storyofstuff.org—one group's effort to invite and encourage exactly that kind of reflection as we consider what to buy or eat or bring into our homes. You might try researching the backstory of the sofa you love to lie on (in your many leisure hours) or a silk dress or the electronic device in your pocket. A lot of processes converge there, and human stories that lie mostly hidden. Try writing your own story of a piece of stuff, acknowledging complicating factors and the choice points, risks, pressures, social and economic forces at work.

* * *

A line in T. S. Eliot's "Burnt Norton" haunts me from time to time, "What might have been and what has been / point to one end, which is always present." We carry the "might have been" with us. It surfaces like a thread here and there in the weave of the days we live in "real time." What I have learned from Eliot and others is that hypotheticals matter. It's good not to get stuck in "What if?" but it's also good to ask the question from time to time, if only to remind ourselves of constant possibility. How things happen has something to do with how things might have happened. The "might have" exerts a certain pressure on the actual. So try going hypothetical: pursue a few questions like these:

What might happen?
What could happen?
What would happen if I changed this one thing?
How might I change what's happening right now?
What would it take to change the course of what's happening?

These are questions not only to ask yourself as you plot your story, but occasionally to raise with the reader explicitly in one way or another, either through a character's speculations or perhaps in the musings of the narrator as they face their "dear reader" and invite them to reflect.

* * *

As you consider how things happen, make space for mystery and minutiae. Think about the "butterfly effect" as explained for us all by the kindly staff at Wikipedia: "The term butterfly effect is closely associated with the work of Edward Lorenz, who spoke about how the formation and path of a tornado might be influenced by minor perturbations such as a far distant butterfly flapping its wings." Think about how each of the following phrases introduces or allows for a similar sort of mystery.

"In the fullness of time, it came to pass . . ."
"I . . . found myself . . . within view of the melancholy House of Usher"
"Out of quiet thunderclap he would abrupt (man, horse, demon) upon a scene . . ."
Once upon a time there were . . .
And then an angel appeared . . . a miracle occurred . . . the heavens opened and a voice was heard.

Try this: Write a paragraph exploring what might happen, or what might have happened, to change outcomes. You might start with one of these, for instance:

If I hadn't been late that day . . .
It's possible one morning she will wake up and find she's ready . . .

> *Before that can happen a critical mass of people will need to . . .*

...

Once again, let's see what we can learn from how writers who play with causality. This first example is from a delightful story by Grace Paley called "Wants."

> In many ways, he said, as I look back, I attribute the dissolution of our marriage to the fact that you never invited the Bertrams to dinner.
>
> That's possible, I said. But really, if you remember: first, my father was sick that Friday, then the children were born, then I had those Tuesday-night meetings, then the war began. Then we didn't seem to know them anymore. But you're right. I should have had them to dinner.

Notice the comic effect of Paley's compressing long-separated events of different orders of importance into a simple, spare sequence, and how it puts us at a wildly unfamiliar "altitude" relative to the events of the life being recalled. Time distortions of the opposite kind—representing what are usually brief, quick processes in slow motion—can have a similar thought-provoking, disorienting effect.

...

In *V for Vendetta*, Alan Moore upends the logic of blame by reassigning the cause of distressing large-scale developments in public life to the one complaining about them. The technique is not altogether unfamiliar: various psychotherapeutic methods similarly pose the question, "What was your role in what happened to you?" They make the useful point that to some degree many personal victim narratives aren't quite objective enough to fairly account for the collusions we may enter passively or unconsciously. As in the previous example, the surprising shift of scale in this passage makes a dramatic point that we are likely participants in processes we think of as both impersonal and inflicted.

> Where once you had the freedom to object, to think and speak as you saw fit, you now have censors and systems of surveillance coercing your conformity and soliciting your submission. How did this happen? Who's to blame? Well certainly there are those more responsible than others, and they will be held accountable, but again truth be told, if you're looking for the guilty, you need only look into a mirror. I know why you did it. I know you were afraid. Who wouldn't be? War, terror, disease. There were a myriad of problems which conspired to corrupt your reason and rob you of your common sense.

Uncomfortable as it may make the reader, this confrontation comes like a dousing of cold water as the writer "breaks the fourth wall" and confronts the reader directly: "I know why you did it." We're no longer in a take-it-or-leave-it relationship to the information content the writer has offered, or the analysis, but are being put vicariously into a moment of self-awareness and self-confrontation. We are called to self-examination and possibly repentance. Maybe our notions of sin or social evil are being reframed. A lot is going on in that apparently incidental shift of direction, including a reassessment of perhaps too easy assumptions about causes and effects.

* * *

I want to offer a final example that may be useful to those of you who want to reflect on public history in your memoirs or essays. Historiography—how history is told—seems to me endlessly interesting. Like novelists, but with greater constraints, historians have to keep firmly in mind what they are committed to being faithful to. The available documentation? A particular well-defined perspective? The multiplicities of perspective offered by other historians and journalists? The marginalized, unwritten stories generally omitted by historians who represent the perspectives of the "victors"?

When we tell the history of anything, personal or political, we navigate a plethora of possibilities at every step. Wikipedia articles offer interesting examples of writing that attempt to give an "overview," a short history, a usable and fair account, of what's most essential to know about a subject. A Wikipedia entry isn't meant to be exhaustive, but to offer a reliable starting point for further research and thought. Consider some of the choices the writer of these paragraphs about Hitler's rise to power made in representing how something as enormous and consequential as the Third Reich happened.

> Adolf Hitler's rise to power began in Germany in September 1919 when Hitler joined the political party then known as the Deutsche Arbeiterpartei (DAP). The name was changed in 1920 to the Nationalsozialistische Deutsche Arbeiterpartei—NSDAP (National Socialist German Workers' Party, commonly known as the Nazi Party). It was anti-Marxist and opposed to the democratic post-war government of the Weimar Republic and the Treaty of Versailles, advocating extreme nationalism and Pan-Germanism as well as virulent anti-Semitism. Hitler attained power in March 1933, after the Reichstag adopted the Enabling Act of 1933 in that month, giving expanded authority. President Paul von Hindenburg had already appointed Hitler as Chancellor on 30 January 1933 after a series of parliamentary elections and associated backroom intrigues. The Enabling Act—when used ruthlessly and with authority—virtually assured that Hitler could thereafter constitutionally exercise dictatorial power without legal objection.
>
> Hitler rose to a place of prominence in the early years of the party. Being one of its best speakers, he was made leader after he threatened to leave otherwise. He was aided in part by his willingness to use violence in advancing his political objectives and to recruit party members who were willing to do the same. The Beer

Hall Putsch in November 1923 and the later release of his book *Mein Kampf* (My Struggle) expanded Hitler's audience. In the mid-1920s, the party engaged in electoral battles in which Hitler participated as a speaker and organizer, as well as in street battles and violence between the Communist's Rotfrontkämpferbund and the Nazis' Sturmabteilung (SA). Through the late 1920s and early 1930s, the Nazis gathered enough electoral support to become the largest political party in the Reichstag, and Hitler's blend of political acuity, deceptiveness, and cunning converted the party's non-majority but plurality status into effective governing power in the ailing Weimar Republic of 1933.

Once in power, the Nazis created a mythology surrounding their rise to power.

Notice the definitive starting point, the range of official acts and treaties mentioned, and the official groups involved. Notice also how the writer singles out one of Hitler's conspicuous skills—his rhetorical effectiveness—as a major contributing cause. And then, at the end of the passage quoted, the acknowledgment that the Nazis' own history was effectively a "mythology." The relationship between history and myth in any national narrative is its own large topic. It may be that one of your tasks as a family or public historian will be to demythologize a narrative that has left out complicating factors whose hearing may prove to be healing.

It's hard not to mythologize or sentimentalize or veer to make our narratives fit preconceived patterns—others' notions, or our own, about what "good story" looks like. It's hard not to fall into familiar grooves when we account for how things have happened. As you look around at the historical moment we're living in, consider some of the language journalists, news anchors, politicians, and others use to describe it:

unprecedented
apocalyptic

tipping point
cataclysmic (from Greek, "to wash down," reference to deluge or flood)
catastrophic (from Greek, "down turning," later sudden turning or overturning)
decision point (from Latin, "to cut off")
paradigm shift (from Greek, "pattern")
not normal / "new normal"
surreal
transition (from Latin, "crossing over")

These terms in various ways underscore the notion that we're in a moment of precarious change—collective, global, and paradigmatic. They single out this moment in history as one that is different from other moments of significant social, or geopolitical, shifts. Consider language you yourself use when you talk over the news—the wars, the elections, climate change, AI, viruses, and self-driving cars.

At the same time, consider the language you tend to use to describe similar moments of change in personal history after loss or displacement or disruption:

entering a new chapter
starting over
regrouping
reframing
in a transition
reassessing
renewing, restoring
disorienting (where are the new boundaries?)
investigating, questioning
opening
taking stock

As you look at the list, consider which terms seem most descriptive of the period you're living in or writing about. Why might one descriptor be more adequate than another? What might you, in your word choice, be hoping to defend or spin positively or clarify? How do your word choices reflect your own sense of responsibility as well as causality?

Sometimes a metaphor helps convey not only the situation you're describing, but the feeling that goes with it. Consider the logic and implications of these common metaphors for the kinds of transition periods mentioned above:

on a precipice
riding a wave
swimming far from shore
in freefall
in a dark wood
on a winding path
in the fog

Each of those expressions implies its own kind of dilemma or challenge, its own quality of anxiety or bewilderment, its own possible resolution. A precipice implies one of three choices: jump, rappel down, or back away from it and find a safe path down the other side. Riding a wave suggests that if you manage the moment with skill and alertness, even a strong, wild wave will bring you to shore and safety. If you're in the fog, you can wait where you are until it lifts or go slowly, feeling your way.

In all the transitional situations alluded to here, several questions remain pertinent as you consider how to narrate the story you have to tell:

What am I (are we) at the end of?
What am I (are we) in the middle of?
What am I (are we) at the beginning of?
What do I (we) hope for?

* * *

In even the simplest narrative, the time dimension remains mysterious. It's relatively easy to think about how the past leads to the present or the present to the future, but think about how these propositions might also be true:

> The past is not dead. It's not even past.
>
> —William Faulkner

> The past keeps changing.
>
> —Chana Bloch

> The future is a faded song.
>
> —T. S. Eliot

> Time is an illusion.
>
> —Albert Einstein

> All is always now.
>
> —T. S. Eliot

> The present is the point at which time touches eternity.
>
> —C. S. Lewis

> Time moves in one direction, memory in another.
>
> —William Gibson

> They say time changes things, but you actually have to change them yourself.
>
> —Andy Warhol

> No people whose word for "yesterday" is the same as their word for "tomorrow" can be said to have a firm grip on time.
>
> —Salman Rushdie

* * *

Anyone who has compared memories with an adult sibling knows there are variant versions of the way it was. We can be sure that, to some degree, however faithful we try to be to how things happened, we're going to tell it the way it wasn't. Still, our memories, however inaccurate, remain with us, recorded, as we now know, in our very cells. They shape us. They don't have to determine our behavior: forgiveness is powerful; release of old resentments is freeing. But what has been remains a part of what is. This is as true for characters in fiction as for the self you portray in memoir. The fears overcome, the freedoms claimed, affirmations or criticisms internalized—all remain factors in present character and behavior patterns.

We carry the past as a source of wisdom along with its burden of regret. Regret is, arguably, pointless. So are nostalgia and wistfulness and guilt that lingers after forgiveness. But there can be value in recognizing and considering both what has been and what might have been as a dimension of ongoing consciousness, both invitations to remember what might still be. And the past is malleable: we know we can reframe disasters as moments from which great good emerged.

* * *

The future exerts its own pressure on stories that move through the past to the present. When we speculate, prognosticate, worry, hope, or simply imagine possibilities, we're acknowledging our present involvement with what hasn't yet happened. Think about how "futurizing" shapes your own life story. We try to imagine (or strenuously avoid imagining) the adaptations we'll have to keep making to climate change. We speculate about the outcomes and consequences of our own and other countries' elections. We wonder what might be the long-term effects of species extinctions or pesticides in foods or AI. We're not sure what we're preparing for—or being prepared for. The open page is an image of the open future. We're always writing into the unknown. Unwritten sentences belong to the future that keeps opening new portals.

* * *

Lyric poems and occasional paragraphs within narratives can create pauses in the forward movement of time and invite and allow us to burrow more deeply into the present. To write presently is not to move on—not just yet—but to alight, hover, burrow, circle, or drill into the present. We have the voices of poets and philosophers to help us do that. Notions like simultaneity, synchronicity, and "the eternal now" can give us language for "nowness." In *Four Quartets* T. S. Eliot offers a sustained reflection on "the intersection of the timeless with time," claiming in the line quoted above, "*All is always now.*"

"There is no single way it can be told." It could be otherwise. We'll never give a full accounting for how things happen, any more than any of us really can tell "the whole truth." Competing narratives may be "true" in different ways—true to different understandings of what matters. To write with this awareness is to foster the great writerly virtue Keats called "negative capability"—the capacity of the "poetic mind" to dwell in ambiguity or paradox without "straining after resolution." Once we give up "resolution," we can choose a thread and spin out that story in ways that allow us to see, with luminous clarity or surprising complexity, one true thing.

FACE FACTS

I believe that there is a kind of poetry,
even a kind of truth, in simple fact.

—Edward Abbey

I'm colder now.
Evenings are darker.
No one calls.
The last leaf has fallen.

A simple series of facts like these can affect us like poetry. They give us scenes and sensations to remember and evoke feelings with those memories. Facts invite inference. They establish grounding points and give us time-space referents. An old TV detective, Jack Webb, would famously say as he gathered information from witnesses, "Just the facts, ma'am. Just the facts." But not many of us want "just the facts." We want the story. We want to know how the facts string together. We want to know how we know they're facts. We want to kick at them like tires and make sure they hold up to skeptical scrutiny.

Facts aren't just for research papers or newsfeeds (though we might wish more newsfeeds would stick to them). Facts are essential for fiction. Sometimes a fact finds its way into a poem. Facts act like seeds: they sit in your hand small and dry and drab until you plant them in a paragraph and let them grow. I recommend you scatter them liberally in whatever you write. Often a fact changes the frame.

All facts come with implications and raise at least two questions: (1) If that's true, what else might be true? and (2) If that's true, what else do I need to know to put it in the right context? Most of them raise a third question, a little more personal and possibly uncomfortable: (3) If that's true, what does it behoove me to do about it? (And I pause here to say it gives me particular pleasure to write sentences that actually require the word *behoove.*)

Here's a fact, for example: Fungi play a key role in cleaning the planet by decomposing dead organic matter. Did we know that? Do we care? And how is it relevant to the love story I'm writing? Let's try out one of our questions: If that's true, what else might be true?

- The planet needs cleaning. If things didn't decompose we'd all die.
- We're surrounded with living beings, including weird, inconspicuous thread-like fungal networks that are working for us and with us. They are our neighbors.
- They help take care of us. We depend on them. Maybe we need to take care of them. Which means taking care of the soil they live in.
- It would be a good idea to find out what chemical pesticides do to soil and fungi. And maybe to stop using those pesticides.

By the time we get to the fourth point, we're in a wider place of reflection. If the conversation continues, it will likely take a political or theological or culinary or ethical turn. We might make a point about how to regulate pesticides for the sake of public health. We might reflect for a while on the fact that if we think of nonhuman beings as our "neighbors," we will develop a profoundly different, more enlivening, relationship with the world around us. We might also, if we're inclined to write about food, pivot to talking about the various fungi we eat, how versatile and pervasive, and also tasty, they are. We might stop writing and make mushroom soup.

Notice what happens when you drop a fact into a story, say about a woman struggling with the challenges of early motherhood:

> It was hard enough for her to get through the store with two toddlers in the cart, let alone scanning labels for HFCS [high-fructose corn syrup], hidden—and she couldn't unlearn this—in 74% of packaged foods. Food literacy might keep her children healthy, but every new food fact she learned made her anxious. It made her want to emigrate. Or live off the grid. She sighed and put the big box of cereal back on the shelf. Both boys wailed.

We might want to know more about this woman. And about high-fructose corn syrup. Reading about her moment in the supermarket, we may find ourselves admiring or sympathizing with or smirking at the problems of the privileged classes. In any case, that 74 percent is a bit of learning we, too, may realize we can't unlearn.

Imagine a story, fiction or nonfiction, that might emerge around any of these facts:

- Over one and a half million people work for Amazon.
- Hummingbirds use spiderwebs to bind their nests together.
- Plastics didn't come into common consumer use until after World War II.

As you consider each of those facts, imagine your way into a story: What might a day in the life of an Amazon worker look like? Could they have gotten another job? How much time do they have for lunch? Or ask yourself, What might happen in a children's story about a hummingbird and a spider? Or, how might my grandmother have responded when she first had a choice between a plastic food container and one made of metal or glass?

It's good, I have found, to start a writing session now and then with a statistic. Or a fact. I used to walk into my writing class, greet all my aspiring (or reluctant) writers, and inscribe a fact or statistic like one of the following on the board:

- It can take up to three liters of water to make a disposable half-liter plastic water bottle.
- On average, Americans consume about three pounds of sugar per week.
- More than one in ten Americans have no health insurance.
- "Roughly, for the price of a single Hawk bomber, the government could provide one and a half million people with clean drinking water for life" (Arundahti Roy, *War Talk*).

The assignment was to consider one of two questions: (1) If this fact is true, what else is likely to be true? Or (2) If this is true, what more might I need to know to respond meaningfully?

For the purpose of the exercise, I suggested we simply assume that the fact was reasonably reliable and verifiable. The students were invited to spend three minutes writing a response to one of the questions. Time enough for a few sentences. A tiny part of the day. What I hoped for in that little exercise was habit formation. It's good to start now and then with a statistic or fact just to see where it takes you.

Some statistics are so shocking, they seem to "speak for themselves"—but they don't, really. They need to be illustrated, contextualized, framed and reframed, reflected upon. Their implications need to be spelled out. They need context and comment. Numbers need to be translated into faces. Any one of the above statements opens a box of questions at least as big as Pandora's.

I remember one morning, before a new wave of military action was unleashed in the Middle East, an interview on *Democracy Now!* in which Amy Goodman asked a human rights lawyer to spell out *what it means* to have, as Gazans did, only two to four hours of electricity per day. He gave a list: sewage treatment plants can't work, so tons of sewage go into public waters and the ocean. Water can't be delivered to consumers with any regularity. With no refrigeration, meat becomes inedible. Hospitals can deliver only a fraction of normal services. People on ventilators can't breathe.

A list like that, which opens up the implications of a single fact, helps us begin to imagine the many-stranded stories that lie behind what really can't be called a "simple" fact. We begin to want to do something: Find a human rights organization and help out. Call a legislator. Donate. Write. Until our imaginations are engaged, it's hard to act with energy, passion, commitment, or intelligence.

I recommend the regular practice of poking at a fact for three minutes. You might begin the process with any of these, for instance:

This fact alone suggests . . .
To put this in context, we need to consider . . .
This fact raises important questions about . . .

It's good to check the fact, for sure—cross-check, find sources you trust, ask friends about theirs. But then, once you have hold of a credible fact, it's good to sit with it long enough to see how it might actually change your mind and your world. And the stories you have to tell.

Once you find out how much water is wasted bottling water, you might think twice about buying the next flat of water for the company picnic. Once you find out that one out of three children in North America is likely to develop diabetes, you might decide to help your kids (and their teachers) reframe what a "treat" looks like.

There are no "simple" facts. All facts are fountainheads. Find one and sit with it. See where it takes you. Go there!

IF YOU WRITE PROSE, TRY POETRY

If a writer works in more than one genre, the chances of getting writer's block are greatly diminished.

—Marge Piercy

Virginia Woolf claimed that one of the most important things a writer needed to think about was rhythm. This idea surprised me—writers have so much else to think about. But the more I thought back over the writers I most admire, the more I realized every one of them conveys a vivid sense of musicality. Each of them developed a kind of signature rhythm, as recognizable after reading a fair sample of their work as a few bars of Bach or Bob Dylan. The difference between prose and poetry isn't simply a categorical or structural difference, but a difference in what features of language they call to our attention—a difference not only of purpose but of evocative possibilities. Prose and poetry require different things of us as readers and stretch us in different directions as writers.

I'll go out on a limb and say here that I don't think we can write good prose without some practice of poetry. I've written elsewhere about poetry as a practice, as a way of caring for language itself, so I won't repeat all I said there (In *Caring for Words in a Culture of Lies* and in *Speaking Peace in a Climate of Conflict*) but will focus in this chapter on how poetic devices help you fine-tune the ways you use and listen to words. Even if you don't write verse, crafting sentences with close attention to cadence and sound, and familiarizing yourself with poetic devices and figures of speech, is good exercise.

It quickens the sense memory and deepens the delight you already take in words—which you do, or you wouldn't be a writer.

I'd call Walt Whitman's poetry prosy. I'd call Annie Dillard's prose poetic. Charles Simic and Claudia Rankine, among others, have written prose poems that are clearly, as writer Amanda Johnston put it, "more than a paragraph." Prose poems might look like paragraphs, but they call emphatic attention to rhythm, sound, related imagery; they make sidelong moves and surprising metaphorical leaps. They invite us to think poetically and remind us that poetry is a way of seeing, receiving, and articulating experience that is never simply linear.

Prose may be more or less poetic. Lab reports are not especially poetic. Almost any paragraph from one of Toni Morrison's novels, or even her essays, is. An interesting place for any writer to work is in the borderland between prose and poetry. It's a "riparian zone" where, as in the biological world, land and water meet and different species interact. Riparian zones are both protective and generative. Things happen there that can't happen in other established ecosystems. And surprising things happen at the riparian edge where poetry meets prose.

Here are some things that can happen when your prose veers into poetic territory: it will look different. It will sound different. It will remap familiar trains of thought. It will slow you down. And wake you up. What happens may seem less important than how it feels to hear about it. Take a look at how this prose-poem by Bruce Holland Rogers does its work, for instance:

YELLOWSTONE BURNING

For the second time today I find myself stepping into traffic against the light. Tires squeal, and a sedan stops an arm's length from my knees. It has been like this all week. All week I have felt like Yellowstone burning. Above smoke-shrouded mountains, the sun dims with the shifting wind. Fire advances along the ridgeline

> of my spine, and trees explode like drums of turpentine with an orange flash and a ball of black smoke. Helicopters hover to take on water, their blades beating the bitter air. Ashes snow down. The moose and bear and elk move on ahead of the flames, but the ground squirrels dodge from rock to tree until they are surrounded. Beneath my skin, nests crackle like candy wrappers.

Notice how the time and space frames shift from one sentence to the next. How it foregrounds subjectivity: the way things happen seems to have little to do with causality. How an exterior scene becomes surreal and dreamlike by means of a metaphor. How the matter-of-fact tone becomes progressively more at odds with the fantastic representation of body as landscape. How you are left not with a street scene or with memories of Yellowstone, but with a sense of what it feels like to be in an extreme state of mind or being.

In that spirit, try writing a few sentences that take us from outside to inside. Start, as Rogers does, with an incident that triggers a feeling or memory. Appropriate, as he does, a metaphor for what it feels like inside—a day with darkening clouds and then torrential rain, for instance, or a stretch of beach disappearing at high tide. See where it takes you in four or five sentences.

* * *

Just as poetry can move in the direction of prose, so prose can move in the direction of poetry. I recently read two books written for young adults—one a play, one a novel—in verse. In both the writers used a succession of simple, short lines to take us deep into the complexities of scene and character. Reading them, I had the feeling that the vertical dimension had overtaken the horizontal left-to-right dimension of language. As I moved down the page following short lines that were often phrases, feelings accumulated, layered visually on top of each other. The reading experience was quite different from what happens when I read a paragraph—even a very good one—in prose, but also different in length and development from most poems I know.

The simplest way to experiment with that intermediate discursive space is to lay your sentences out differently: phrase them out. Without trying to make what you've written sound "like a poem," just separate phrases and put them on successive lines. Make stanza breaks where you feel like it. Then see what happens.

Try this: Write three sentences, one starting with a preposition, one with an imperative (*Look! Listen . . .*), and one with *I* or *you*. Once you have your three sentences, break them into phrases—lay them out like a poem and see what happens. Here's an example:

> Up the beach a child is filling a pail with sand.
> Watch—when it's full she will pour it out and begin again.
> You did that; I never understood why.

Let's give it poetic form:

> Up the beach
> a child is filling
> a pail with sand.
>
> Watch—when it's full
> she will pour it out
> and begin again.
>
> You did that.
> I never understood why.

Something happens to the prose sentences when they are separated into parts. What the parts do by themselves seems to matter more. The effects of phrases become more apparent.

* * *

There are other easy ways to make your prose move in the direction of poetry. For instance, name one thing—an observation, an object, the feeling of a moment, a quality of light, etc.:

> The room is growing cold.

Consider what that one thing constellates—associations, logical connections, similar sounds:

> So like evenings in Edinburgh,
> but without a crackling fire in the stove.

Choose a path to travel for at least a couple of lines or for a sentence:

> Not much romance in bleak midwinter,
> not much to sing about,

Change camera angles:

> though the consolations of song
> saw my grandmother through
> nights in the Yukon with two
> shivering boys and no wood.

Stay grounded in the five senses (avoid abstractions unless they're necessary to your purpose):

> By the time she sang to me, rocking
> in the faded rose-colored chair she loved

Allow your purpose to reveal itself:

> she had made her peace with hardship
> and made her hard way south.

She sang by open windows.
Summer evenings were long.

Pay attention to sound and rhythm:

All of them sounded like hymns:
"Just as I am, I come."
"I come to the garden alone."

Play with line breaks, stanza breaks, syntax:

We rocked
        until sleep came,
                always to me,
                        sometimes to her, as well.

Notice where it wants to go:

Nothing was warmer
than that voice,
even in midwinter.
I hum her hymns now
when it's cold.

Don't crowd the words. Give each word space to breathe.

* * *

One practice I recommend is to work from simple prompts—a word, another word, and a third word—and see what comes. Start a sequence of three sentences, for instance, with *outside*, *inside*, *tomorrow*. See if, in those three sentences, some thread of story can be suggested, or a mood or feeling. See if you can enhance that mood or feeling with line breaks:

Outside the late light softens.
Inside I leave the lamps unlit.
Tomorrow the journey begins
for which the coming darkness
is preparation.

Or do a similar exercise with three kinds of sentences—an imperative, a simple observation, and an I or you statement, for instance:

Come to the table.
All is made ready.
You are my guest.

* * *

One of the most conspicuous devices that separates poetic discourse from prose is giving visible form to the words on the page. Rhymed verses, unrhymed blank verse that follows a regular rhythmic pattern, and free verse, which puts the poetic line in creative tension with the sentence as a unit of meaning, can all be easily distinguished from a prose paragraph. Each of those forms has its own "rules"—we recognize sonnets, villanelles, odes, and limericks by particular meters and line lengths. Each of these forms organizes the way we take in impressions and information and guides us to stop in unusual places and hear the momentary silence of empty page space before moving to the next line.

Simply taking a few sentences of prose and "phrasing them out"—laying them on the page phrase by phrase in vertical succession—can help you see and, more importantly, hear your own words differently as you give them poetic form by the simple device of line breaks. You'll begin to see where little bits of word clutter may be taking energy away from a strong, vivid verb or image. You'll see where to prune. And you'll begin to hear and see the natural rhythms and range of your sentences, your habits of modification, your sense of sound. Notice, for example, what happens when I take the following ordinary prose sentences and phrase them out:

> Some plants thrive even in the worst heat of summer. They seem brave out there, staying green and glistening in all that sunlight. Others are wilting. We bring the smaller ones inside to protect them, water the rest, and live in trust that rain will pass this way again.

> Some plants thrive
> even in the worst
> heat of summer.
> They seem brave
> out there, staying green
> and glistening
> in all that sunlight.

> Others are wilting.
> We bring the smaller ones
> inside to protect them,
> water the rest,
> and live in trust
> that the rain
> will pass this way again.

Those sentences didn't suddenly turn into a luminous and finished poem, but they do land differently, if only by cueing us to register each single phrase as a thought or feeling in its own right. Try phrasing out a few of your own sentences and see what happens. You may be your own best teacher as you look for places to bring out the poetry in your prose.

Even though they're not the dominant forms of poetry at this point, there's value in working with fixed forms just to notice the effects of the rhythms that reflect the "drumbeats" of the language. Iambic pentameter—da-DAH, da-DAH, da-DAH, da-DAH, da-DAH—has lasted through the centuries since Shakespeare and Milton wrote sonnets partly because it's an easy, natural rhythm for

English speakers to fall into: "I **think** I'll **go** and **buy** a **loaf** of **bread**" or "Give **me** the **keys**; I **want** to **take** the **car**" are simple English sentences in perfect iambic pentameter.

Plenty of handbooks and online sites provide inventories of verse forms (i.e. villanelle, ghazal, ode, ballad) and metric rhythms (i.e., iamb, spondee, trochee, anapest, dactyl) in English poetry, so I'm not going to do that here, except to say it's worth learning at least the most common of them like dance steps. You can move around a dance floor without instruction, but dance is a lot more fun and more beautiful if you know a few basic moves.

An important poetic dimension of prose is sound patterns, alliteration and assonance being two of the most commonly recognized—repetition of initial consonants and repetition of internal vowel sounds. Either can be overused and become trivial or tedious, but used judiciously they can be a joy to hear. Think, for instance, of the opening lines of Shelley's "Ode to the West Wind":

> O wild West Wind, thou breath of Autumn's being,
> Thou, from whose unseen presence the leaves dead
> Are driven, like ghosts from an enchanter fleeing . . .

Antique as the language is, it still has the power to move and awaken us to a sense of Presence in the natural forces around us. These three lines achieve their effect by means not only of alliteration and assonance but also of repeated rhythm, personification, simile, and metaphor. All that in three lines. To point out all these devices isn't to say simple multiplication of poetic devices adds value, but to recognize that skillful, conscious use of them can add depth and dimension to what a sentence can do in either prose or verse.

• • •

Onomatopoeia—using words like *buzz* or *crack* or *bubble* that sound like what they mean—awakens a felt sense of meaning, adding a dimension to straightforward left-brain cognition. You might, in fact, think of poetry as a form of writing that is deliberate and strategic about activating the left brain and the right brain simultaneously: meaning, a poet might say, must be felt as well as understood. Try writing a few sentences or lines in which sound patterns are conspicuous enough to add a noticeable layer of feeling to the information the lines convey. Something like this, for instance:

> The boy watched the baby, asleep in her bassinet, and wondered what it would mean to be a brother.

> The hum of the dishwasher and buzz of the neighbor's chainsaw cheered her somehow as she drank tea and deliberated.

Those devices play with sound effects. Other devices deliver meaning in distinct ways. Irony, allusion, paradox, and metaphor are like the various ways a skilled pitcher can get a ball over the plate, or the ways a skilled tennis player can aim, place, and put spin on the ball. The effectiveness of these devices depends in part on an awareness of audience: how you deliver your message or cue your readers to think twice and teach them not to take all things literally depends on imagining the readers you hope for. If you want them to be thoughtful, pitch them a few paradoxes that require them to pause and consider how "the opposite is also true."

Or help them feel the ironic distance between a character's inflated claims about their own charitable efforts and the experience of another character who lives in poverty and knows just where those efforts run aground.

Or if you're speaking about the complexities of peacemaking in a culture of violence, a phrase taken from Lincoln's Second Inaugural Address—"with malice toward none, with charity for all"—can situate your observations against a wide historical backdrop and offer some measure of how the conduct of war and warfare has changed.

Biblical writings offer valuable examples of all of these: Jesus used poetic devices regularly, doubtless different in Hebrew and

Aramaic, but whose effects survive into English: "Yet wisdom is justified by all her children." "Whoever finds his life will lose it, and whoever loses his life for my sake will find it." "I am the bread of life." "I am the vine." "Everyone who hears these words of mine and does them will be like a wise man who built his house on the rock." Of course, none of those texts was written in English. It's fun and instructive, though, to notice how many biblical passages are rendered as poetry and include poetic devices and wordplay familiar to English speakers, partly because scholars recognize a rich range of poetic devices and wordplay in the original Hebrew. Most translations try to represent the Hebrew poetry of the psalms with some English equivalent. Passages that might have been chanted or sung are treated differently than prose.

All together, biblical texts offer a wide, fascinating variety of "ways of putting it." I mention it here because the Bible is a treasury of different discourses—poetry, prophecy, history, myth, annals, letters, biography—and underscores the truth that there is "no single way it can be told." That some of it is poetry is a clear testimony to the fact that deep truths can't be adequately articulated without it.

* * *

Paradox heightens our awareness of the ways in which, so often, the opposite is also true: the rich are poor; power is vulnerability; saying no may be a way of saying yes. Every spiritual tradition or teacher I know of resorts to paradox to get at what is true, since truth is never one-sided. It helps us turn what we have normalized to new angles and make it strange—a move Adrienne Rich claimed was a primary task of the poet. A simple way to practice paradox is to try flipping commonplaces upside down. Try a paragraph or short list of ways any of these paradoxes might be true:

> Sometimes protection puts us in danger.
> Having less is a way of having more.
> It takes a long time for adults to become childlike.

Some pleasures come only from discomfort.
It sometimes takes courage to do nothing.

* * *

Metaphor is an indispensable human way of knowing. Practicing using and developing metaphors effectively is one of the most worthwhile things you can do as a writer of poetry or prose or, indeed, as a speaker or just as someone who wants to make conversation lively. Metaphor is a way of weaving the world together, seeing how one thing is like and not like another, and how all things in the created order exist in relationship. One can get quite mystical about it, but I will forgo that here and just invite you to think about and play with metaphors before we continue. Consider, for instance, the range of things apt metaphors can do:

they reframe
they subvert clichés
they surprise us into seeing familiar things in unfamiliar ways
they activate the imagination
they offer their own irreducible information

* * *

In "Of Modern Poetry" Wallace Stevens inventories what poetry must do to be sufficient to its task:

It has to be living, to learn the speech of the place.
It has to face the men of the time and to meet
The women of the time. It has to think about war
And it has to find what will suffice.
It must
Be the finding of a satisfaction.

I'd like to linger momentarily on that last word. *Satisfaction* is a modest word, but, in its understated way, it recalls the biblical promise that our deepest hunger will be "satisfied." It has a surprising sufficiency when we see it in the context of Eliot's magi recalling their discovery of the Christ child: "It was, you may say, satisfactory." To be satisfied, to find what is sufficient, is specifically not to be indulged or flooded with excess, but to find that a need may be so precisely met that it gives way to contentment.

The practice of poetry, even for prose writers, even for those who write only in journals sequestered in locked drawers, invigorates the mind and keeps the heart open. Dangling out there in white space, those words at the ends of lines make themselves heard and give us pause. The rhythms poets find, like those of jazz drummers, align our own heartbeats to others' and train the sensibilities that lie just beneath our defensive intellectual radar. They are not, Audre Lorde insisted, a luxury, but an instrument of awareness and even, sometimes, of survival. In her book *Saved by a Poem*, Kim Rosen writes about hearing poetry in "refugee camps, war-torn countries, homeless shelters, prisons, and post-disaster sites." People in the direst situations read it, write it, put themselves at some risk to hear it. The needs it meets aren't always easy to identify until, suddenly, with shocking consolation, they are met.

KNOW WHEN TO STOP

A crucial decision about a piece of writing is where to end it. Often the story will tell you where it wants to stop.

—William Zinsser

"'And so,' as Tiny Tim observed, 'God bless us every one.'" It's not a bad idea to end a story with a blessing. You can go bleak, as Orwell does in *1984*, thwarting our hope that the protagonist will prevail against the political machine: "He loved big brother." Or you can be blunt to the point of dismissiveness like Dostoyevsky: "That might be the subject of a new story, but our present story is ended." Or you can make the end a beginning, as Isabel Allende does in *House of the Spirits*: "It begins like this: Barrabás came to us by sea. . . ."

There's always more to say. We all know the moment of sadness—a tiny shadow of death—that comes at the end of a novel, or the frustration of wondering what happened then—after the wedding, or the escape, or the verdict. Stories do go on: witness the popularity of sequels and series. Incompletion is inevitable: autobiographies are incomplete by definition, since the writer/subject is still alive to tell the tale. Still, we look for resolution, a mystery solved, the lost found, a wanderer's return, closure—if not a happy ending, at least a satisfactory one without too many unanswered questions left dangling.

In nonfiction, we look for a point of view presented and developed in such a way as to leave us satisfied with, ideally grateful for, what we have learned. We hope for a well-made argument or a story that gives us deeper understanding of others' lives or how public problems might be solved or how things got this way. When we close the book, we hope to be able to speak more knowledgeably and act more effectively in some area that matters.

What you do with the last chapter or paragraph or stanza or sentence matters, but it can matter in a number of ways. Just as some people don't like long good-byes, some prefer a quick, clean conclusion: no sermonizing or moralizing, no general observations or long epilogues. Others, of course, quite like the final address to the reader, the sad acknowledgment that our story is coming to an end, and because of that we may return to our lives a little sadder but wiser for having traveled the road with the author.

Given the range of viable choices, I'm not going to prescribe here, but rather offer a few guidelines to consider as you bring your book or article or poem to completion. What follows are a few thoughts about what makes for a good ending, culled from a long reading life in which some endings remain blazoned on my memory as moments of deep satisfaction and others continue to make me wish irritably for a more plausible or provocative outcome. What makes a good ending is an ongoing discussion that remains lively as the currents of storytelling shift and change in response to the social forces that shape our collective tastes.

* * *

You don't have to resolve everything. The main problem or mystery of course needs to be solved somehow, or at least we need to see some hope of resolution, say, to an oil spill or a family's conflicts. But what happened to minor characters, what happened in a neighboring country or town, or the foreseeable obstacles our protagonists may encounter can remain a matter for readers' private speculation. The critic John Hodgman reminds us that one of the primary reasons readers read stories is because they give shape and sense to much that seems to lack both, and, he adds, "What makes them most comforting is that while life goes on and pain goes on, stories do us the favor of ending." All resolutions are provisional.

* * *

Remind us where we began. Even a slight allusion to the beginning—a place-name, an image—offers a sense of having come full circle. As T. S. Eliot puts it, we "arrive in the place where we started and know it for the first time." The story is now a memory that will mingle with our personal memories and continue to inform them. The beginning of Dante's *Divine Comedy*, "Midway upon the journey of our life I found myself within a forest dark," is alluded to in the final line: "and then we emerged to see the stars again." We have entered and ultimately left a visionary world that will continue to tug at our consciousness as we take up whatever our business is "midway upon the journey" of our own lives.

* * *

Surprise us. Conclusions don't need to be predictable. You're not solving a math problem or logic puzzle; more credibly, you're affirming the ongoingness of all things. So endings may, and perhaps should, come as a bit of a surprise. We may see them coming, but that something new can still happen, or be proposed, in the final paragraph is a refreshing reminder that whether or not this story or line of argument or poetic excursion continues, more is to come. A surprise ending to an argument, for instance, might be an "on the other hand" paragraph. A surprise ending to a mystery might be a new piece of evidence that raises a shadow of a doubt. Or we might be surprised by the speaker in a poem who changes the vantage point, as often happens in the final couplet of a sonnet. Suddenly the speaker in Shakespeare's Sonnet 29 "haply thinks" on the beloved, and the whole mood changes. Many recent narratives that show us how precarious our global situation is, how self-defeating our militarism and intractable our economic inequities are, end with a call to action that offers a glimmer of hope, however modified. Some, indeed, aim to teach us how often hope is "hope for the wrong thing," but how a deeper, different kind of hope is possible.

* * *

Widen the frame. Give us a sense that this relatively insignificant event in a little-known corner of the world mirrors a larger story to which we belong. Or that the point you're making in your op-ed about this mayor's approach to a local problem has wider application. Show us where our stories intersect and resonate and how mythic behavioral patterns continue to recur in ways that show how old stories remain relevant. The final, lovely lines of George Eliot's *Middlemarch* remind us that, though these characters may be long gone, "the growing good of the world is partly dependent on unhistoric acts; and that things are not so ill with you and me as they might have been, is half owing to the number who lived faithfully a hidden life, and rest in unvisited tombs." That number, we feel assured, continues to grow.

* * *

Invite us back. Even if you're not anticipating a sequel or continuing sequence, an ending can be generously hospitable by suggesting that what we have read is part of a much larger, ongoing, engaging conversation that we can now reenter, newly equipped with insights that may change our own perspectives and give us a new authority to speak into the time and place we inhabit. You might, at least obliquely, suggest that a second reading would be worth the time, now that you know what you know.

* * *

Give a benediction. Which means "a good word," or more often, a blessing. In the final stanza of Jane Kenyon's beautiful poem of acceptance, "Let Evening Come," she writes, "God will not leave us / comfortless, so let evening come." It is a restrained reassurance, couched in a double negative. But it gathers us under the shadow of a great wing and gently reminds us that we are in it together—this human condition—and that the glass we see through darkly may well be shading us from a light that awaits us. The words of benediction spoken often in our church as the service ends begin with a similar reminder of mortality: "Life is short, and we do not have too much time to gladden the hearts of those who walk the way with us . . ." But then it continues, "so be swift to love and make haste to be kind," followed by an invocation of God's blessing. Ending in the subjunctive mood—may there be . . . may it be so . . . may you—brings us in a sense face-to-face as fellow humans who live out our stories at the edge of mystery. Your final words may serve, as John O'Donohue puts it, to "bless the space between us."

May all your words be blessings.

AFTERWORD:
SHARPEN YOUR EDITORIAL EYE

Write. Rewrite. When not writing or rewriting, read.
I know of no shortcuts.

—Larry L. King

Once you're "done," it's time to be your own dear reader. Settle in and read your last, best draft—the one you think is nearly ready to send off into the world shining its light. Now is the time to nitpick. Think of it as fine-tuning. Slashing and burning should already have happened as you looked over earlier drafts. Now it's time to think like an editor—polish sentences, tweak and tug and rearrange. See what a surprising difference small adjustments can make.

Do a "vertical reading" of a page or a few paragraphs. Pass your eye down the page, thinking of yourself as a CT scanner seeing successive layers of what's there. The point of a "vertical reading" or what I call a "self-editing scan" is to notice *only* the one pattern as you look over the text in front of you, to see how that feature of your writing looks if you bring it into sharp focus. Seeing a text in layers, so to speak, you begin to see patterns, notice habits, and make more focused decisions about stylistic choices, which are often more consequential than they might seem.

Here are some scans to try—not all at once, but one or two each time you read over portions of your draft. (Or when you're workshopping someone else's writing.) They may sharpen your noticings and help you get to know your own narrative voice or persona better over time.

* * *

Scan for verbs. Just look at the verbs. Are they varied? Precise? Surprising? Repetitive? Do any of them have metaphorical implications (i.e., *she sailed through the room . . .*)?

Notice when you use progressive tense constructions as opposed to simple past. Note tense slippages. Where do you shift from past to present narration and why?

See if you can find a few places to make a verb choice more effective.

* * *

Scan for time markers. Consider how your choice of narrative tense achieves either immediacy or critical distance. How do you establish time frames from one paragraph to the next?

Identify words that offer a sense of time—references to time of day (including, for instance, the angle at which the sun comes in the window) or time of year (for instance, puddles of melted snow underfoot) or time a memory goes back to (i.e., a reference to a stuffed toy).

Notice where simple references to time happen (*It was 9:00 a.m. . . . Sunday morning dawned*) and whether you want to be explicit or more indirect about indicating time.

Notice how simple word tags give a sense of elapsed time: *finally, at length, then, immediately, subsequently . . .*

Consider how movement in time affects the texture and scope of the narrative. How are you inviting your reader to imagine and reflect on time?

* * *

Scan for sentence structure. Where is the energy or weight of the sentence? At the beginning? In the middle, where the verb serves a fulcrum, for instance? At the end, where you finish with a surprising, punchy word choice?

* * *

Scan for sentence starters. Pass your eye down the page just noticing how sentences begin. How many begin with a subject and verb (*He said . . . She laughed . . . They left . . .)*? How many begin with prepositional phrases or modifiers?

How much variation do you see in the ways you begin a sentence? What might more variation serve?

How many sentences begin with "There is" or "There are"? See how many of those you can eliminate in favor of real subjects and verbs.

Similarly, how many begin with a generic pronoun for which the reader will have to look for an antecedent: "This happens when . . ." See if you can name what "this" refers to so the reader doesn't have to do that work.

* * *

Scan for sentence endings. Do sentences end with strong images? Words that have weight? Or do they "trail off" with modifying phrases that don't add much?

* * *

Scan for sentence variation. Are some sentences in a paragraph noticeably shorter than others? If you tend toward long sentences, what are they sustaining? Where might you insert a two-word observation (*That hurt . . . They rose . . .)*? Or where might you combine two sentences to make a more interesting one with a subordinating conjunction?

* * *

Scan for modifiers. How many of them are there? Would more precise verb or noun choices make modifiers less necessary?

If they have metaphorical implications (i.e., *The room was stripped, denuded* . . . or *The talk was crushingly boring*), are the metaphors worth playing out a bit?

Do you occasionally pair a modifier and noun in surprising or paradoxical ways to make an oxymoron (i.e., *Her overbearing calm* . . . *The distressing orderliness* . . .)?

How fitting, surprising, precise, useful, predictable, edgy, or suggestive are they?

* * *

Scan for prepositional phrases. Prepositional phrases are modifiers. See which ones you might eliminate with more concise sentence construction.

Where you need them, consider what they accomplish.

Where do they fall in the sentence, and how do they affect the "energy distribution" or "weight distribution" of the sentence?

Where do they serve to establish camera angle or time frame?

* * *

Scan for abstractions. Some abstractions are inevitable, but remember Ezra Pound's advice to writers: "Go in fear of abstractions."

Scan for words that end in *-tion*, *-ness*, *-ment*, *-ism*, for instance, and see if you can offer an example or image that will stand for the whole concept or movement.

Notice where an abstraction becomes an overgeneralization. Could an example or statistic make the same point? Might an extra sentence refine your point?

* * *

Scan for images. As opposed to abstractions. Where does a word invoke a sense memory? Where do you appeal to the visual imagination? Body sensations? Actual smells or sounds or textures?

How do your verb choices reinforce the images you're working with?

* * *

Scan for metaphors. Where do your images open metaphorical possibilities? Where are they conspicuously and intentionally metaphorical?

* * *

Scan for sounds. Read a passage aloud. Or hear it in your head. Notice the musicality: the alliterations, the assonances, the internal rhyming, the accumulation of *s* sounds or percussive *b* or *t* sounds, and notice the feeling they induce.

* * *

Scan for rhythm/cadence. Read your sentences as you might read lines of poetry—for beat, rhythm, cadence, fluidity, or percussiveness. Where does a sentence or clause have a beat so clear it moves the whole sentence into the foreground of your awareness? To what purpose or effect? When might you work for that effect?

* * *

Scan for allusions. Where do you make any mention, even obliquely, of a biblical story or image, a figure from history or literature or film, a recent news story? How subtle are your allusions? How do they work to your purposes?

* * *

Scan for tonal cues. Where do you shift from serious development of an idea or scene to a moment of humor or reminiscence or ambivalence? How do you mark that? What words or phrases mark tonal shifts?

* * *

Scan for omissions. What have you not done in this scene or chapter or essay or story that you might have been expected to do? What conspicuous omissions are deliberate? Where might you want to go back and insert a paragraph about something you recognize is part of the story you omitted?

Where might it be useful to announce an omission—what you're not going to talk about, for instance, or what names you won't be naming, or what factors you're aware of but won't be taking time to address? Notice how thoroughly or efficiently you handle those omissions.

NOTES ON SOURCES

Read like a Writer

Cohen, Leonard. "Hallelujah." *Various Positions*, 1984. Produced by John Lissauer.
Emerson, Ralph Waldo. "The American Scholar." In *Essays*. Library of America, 1983.
Gafney, Wilda. *Womanist Midrash: A Reintroduction to the Women of the Torah and the Throne*. Westminster John Knox, 2017.
Hemingway, Ernest. *The Sun Also Rises*. Penguin, 2022.
Thoreau, Henry David. *Walden*. Library of America, 2007.
Van Doren, Mark. "Sonnet XXV." In *Collected and New Poems*. 1963.

Begin Beginning

Berry, Wendell. "What We Need Is Here." In *The Collected Poems of Wendell Berry*. 1957–1982. North Point Press, 1987.
Eliot, T. S. "The Dry Salvages." In *Four Quartets*. Ecco, 1991.
Eliot, T. S. "East Coker." In *Four Quartets*. Ecco, 1991.
Eliot, T. S. "Little Gidding." In *Four Quartets*. Ecco, 1991.
"Why Stephen King Spends 'Months and Even Years' Writing Opening Sentences." *Atlantic*, July 23, 2013.
Wolf, Christa. *Patterns of Childhood.* Farrar, Straus & Giroux, 1984.

Move the Camera

Adichie, Chimamanda Ngozi. *Amerikanah*. Vintage, 2013.

Anaya, Rudolfo. *Bless Me, Ultima*. Grand Central Publishing, 2012.
Austen, Jane. *Pride and Prejudice*. Norton, 2016.
Balog, James. *The Human Element: A Time Capsule from the Anthropocene*. Rizzoli, 2021.
Cather, Willa. *My Ántonia*. Norton, 2015.
Collins, Billy. "Why I Don't Keep a Gun in the House." In *The Apple That Astonished Paris*. 1988. University of Arkansas Press, 2014.
Hawthorne, Nathaniel. *The Scarlet Letter*. Norton, 2017.
Kingsolver, Barbara. *Prodigal Summer*. HarperCollins, 2009.
Roy, Arundhati. *The God of Small Things*. Random House, 2008.
Viramontes, Helena María. *Under the Feet of Jesus*. Plume, 1996.

Develop and Digress

Bryson, Bill. *Neither Here Nor There*. HarperCollins, 1993.
Dillard, Annie. *Pilgrim at Tinker Creek*. HarperCollins, 2009.
Lepore, Jill. *These Truths: A History of the United States*. Norton, 2018.
Polti, Georges. *The Thirty-Six Dramatic Situations*. Franklin, OH: James Knapp Reeve, 1916, 1921.

Do the Word Work

Eliot, T. S. "Little Gidding." In *Four Quartets*. Ecco, 1991.

Find Out Who's There

Abulhawa, Susan. *Mornings in Jenin*. Bloomsbury USA, 2010.
Alexander, Michelle. *The New Jim Crow*. New Press, 2020.
Baldwin, James. *Notes of a Native Son*. Penguin, 2017.
Berry, Wendell. *A Memory of Old Jack*. Counterpoint, 1999.
Chomsky, Noam. On Speaking of Democracy. speakingofdemocracy.com. Undated.
Dangarembga, Tsitsi. *Nervous Conditions*. Graywolf, 2021.

Giridharadas, Anand. *Winners Take All.* Vintage, 2018.
Heller, Joseph. *Catch-22*. Global Publishers, 2025.
Lamott, Anne. *Hard Laughter.* North Point Press, 1979.
McCann, Colum. *Apeirogon.* Random House, 2020.
Moraga, Cherrie. "La Guera." In *Loving in the War Years*. Haymarket, 2023.
Morrison, Toni. *Beloved.* Vintage, 2007.
Owen, Wilfred. "Dulce et Decorum Est." In *The Collected Poems of Wilfred Owen*. New Directions, 1965.
Owens, Delia. *Where the Crawdads Sing*. Putnam, 2018.
Roy, Arundhati. *The God of Small Things*. Random House, 2008.
Salinger, J. D. "A Girl I Knew." *Good Housekeeping*, February 1948. (Not included in any of his books.)
Shakespeare, William. *King Lear*. Norton, 2007.
Shipler, David. *The Working Poor*. Knopf, 2004.
Smarsh, Sarah. *Heartland: A Memoir of Working Hard and Being Broke in the Richest Country on Earth*. Scribner, 2018.
Smith, R. Lee. *The Scholomance.* A Red Hot Romance Book, 2012.
Solnit, Rebecca. *The Faraway Nearby.* Penguin, 2013.
Stevenson, Robert Louis. *The Strange Case of Dr. Jekyll and Mr. Hyde.* Reader's Library Classics, 2022.
Vonnegut, Kurt, Jr. *A Man Without a Country*. Dial, 2017.
Whitman, Walt. *Leaves of Grass.* Norton, 2002.
Wiesel, Elie. *Night*. Hill & Wang, 2012.
Zagaziewski, Adam. "Self-Portrait." In *Mysticism for Beginners*. Farrar, Straus & Giroux, 1997.

Get to Know Your Narrator

Fitzgerald, F. Scott. *The Great Gatsby.* Norton, 2021.
Green, John. *Turtles All the Way Down*. Dutton, 2017.
Hawthorne, Nathaniel. *The Scarlet Letter.* Norton, 2017.
McCann, Colum. *Apeirogon*. Random House, 2020.
McEntyre, Marilyn. *Reading like a Serpent*. Cascade, 2012.

Wagamese, Richard. *Embers: One Ojibway's Meditations.* Douglas & McIntyre, 2016.

Zagajewski, Adam. "Try to Praise the Mutilated World." In *Without End: New and Selected Poems.* Farrar, Straus & Giroux, 2002.

Address Your Dear Reader

Brennan, Marie. *A Natural History of Dragons.* Tor Books, 2013.

Brontë, Charlotte. *Jane Eyre.* Norton, 2016.

DiCamillo, Kate. *The Tale of Despereaux.* Candlewick, 2009.

Dostoyevsky, Fyodor. *Notes from Underground.* Wordsworth Editions, 2015.

Dostoyevsky, Fyodor. *White Nights.* Penguin, 2017.

Hoffmann, E. T. A. *The Golden Pot and Other Tales.* Oxford University Press, 2009.

Martin, Judith. *Miss Manners.* Norton, 2011.

Rhimes, Shonda. *Year of Yes.* S&S; Marysue Rucci Books, 2015.

Riordan, Rick. *The Tower of Nero.* Hyperion, 2020.

Setterfield, Diane. *Once upon a River.* Black Swan; Faber & Faber, 2020.

Twain, Mark. *The Innocents Abroad.* Wordsworth Editions, 2010.

Write from Inside Out

Angelou, Maya. *I Know Why the Caged Bird Sings.* Penguin, 2008.

Coates, Ta-Nehisi. *Between the World and Me.* One World, 2015.

Harjo, Joy. *Poet Warrior.* Norton, 2021.

Kingston, Maxine Hong. *The Woman Warrior.* Vintage, 2010.

Norris, Kathleen. *Dakota: A Spiritual Geography.* Mariner Books, 2001.

O'Reilley, Mary Rose. *The Barn at the End of the World: The Apprenticeship of a Quaker Buddhist Shepherd.* Milkweed Editions, 2014.

Shakespeare, William. *King Lear.* Norton, 2007.

Play Along

Chou, Elaine Hsieh. *Disorientation.* Penguin, 2022.
Doyle, Brian. *The Book of Uncommon Prayer.* Sorin Books, 2023.
Duncan, David James. *The Brothers K.* Bantam Doubleday Dell, 1998.
Eliot, T. S. "The Dry Salvages." In *Four Quartets.* Ecco, 1991.
Greer, Germaine. *The Female Eunuch.* Harper, 1970, 2009.
Handey, Jack. *Deep Thoughts.* Grand Central Publishing, 1993.
Lamott, Anne. *Traveling Mercies.* Anchor, 2000.
Nachmanovitch, Stephen. *Free Play: The Power of Improvisation in Life and Art.* Tarcher, 1991.
Patchett, Ann. *These Precious Days.* HarperCollins, 2021.
Satyamurti, Carole. "I Shall Paint My Nails Red." In *Changing the Subject.* Oxford University Press, 1991.
Smith, Zadie. *Swing Time.* Penguin, 2016.
Vowell, Sarah. *The Partly Cloudy Patriot.* Simon & Schuster, 2002.
Wiman, Christian. "Every Riven Thing." In *Every Riven Thing.* Farrar, Straus & Giroux, 2011.
Wong, Ali. *Dear Girls: Intimate Tales, Untold Secrets & Advice for Living Your Best Life.* Random House, 2019.

Tell the Public Part

Asmelash, Leah. "What the Writer of 'We Lived Happily During the War' Wants You to Know About Ukraine." CNN, March 2, 2022. https://tinyurl.com/mptwx6j6.
Coates, Ta Nehisi. *Between the World and Me.* One World, 2015.
Delderfield, R. F. *To Serve Them All My Days.* Sourcebooks Landmark, 2009.
Kaminsky, Ilya. "We Lived Happily During the War." Poetry International Website, © 2013.
Morrison, Toni. *The Bluest Eye.* Vintage, 2007.
Plath, Sylvia. "Lady Lazarus." In *Collected Poems.* HarperCollins, 1981.
Steinbeck, John. *The Grapes of Wrath.* Tingle Books, 2024.

Tell How It Happened

Eliot, T. S. "Burnt Norton." In *Four Quartets*. Ecco, 1991.
Jung, Carl. *Synchronicity: An Acausal Connecting Principle*. Princeton University Press, 2010.
Keats, John. *Complete Poems and Selected Letters of John Keats*. Modern Library, 2001.
Klein, Naomi. *No Is Not Enough*. Haymarket Books, 2017.
Lepore, Jill. *These Truths: A History of the United States*. Norton, 2018.
Levitt, Steven D., and Stephen J. Dubner. *Freakonomics*. William Morrow, 2010.
Lorenz, Edward. Talk given at the American Association for the Advancement of Science, 1972.
Márquez, Gabriel García. *One Hundred Years of Solitude*. HarperCollins, 2006.
Moore, Alan. *V for Vendetta*. DC Comics, 2020.
Paley, Grace. "Wants." In *The Collected Stories*. Farrar, Straus & Giroux, 2007.
Rich, Johnny. *The Human Script*. CreateSpace Independent Publishing Platform, 2013.
Wallace, David Foster. *Infinite Jest*. Little, Brown, 1996.

Face Facts

Abbey, Edward. *Desert Solitaire*. RosettaBooks, 2011.
Roy, Arundahti. *War Talk*. South End Press, 2003.

If You Write Prose, Try Poetry

Eliot, T. S. "The Journey of the Magi." In *T. S. Eliot: The Collected Poems*. Ecco, 1991.
Lincoln, Abraham. "Second Inaugural Address." In *Lincoln's Greatest Speeches*. Independently Published, 2022.

McEntyre, Marilyn. *Caring for Words in a Culture of Lies.* 2nd ed. Eerdmans, 2021.

McEntyre, Marilyn. *Speaking Peace in a Climate of Conflict.* Eerdmans, 2020.

Piercy, Marge. *New York Times*: Writers on Writing, December 20, 1999.

Rogers, Bruce Holland. "Yellowstone Burning." https://tinyurl.com/357cs34f.

Rosen, Kim. *Saved by a Poem.* Hay House, 2009.

Shelley, Percy Bysshe. "Ode to the West Wind." In *Shelley: The Major Works.* Oxford University Press, 2009.

Stevens, Wallace. "Of Modern Poetry." In *The Collected Poems of Wallace Stevens.* Vintage, 2011.

Know When to Stop

Allende, Isabel. *House of the Spirits.* Atria Books, 2015.

Dante. *Divine Comedy.* Oxford University Press, 2008.

Dostoyevsky, Fyodor. *Crime and Punishment.* Norton, 2018.

Eliot, George. *Middlemarch.* Norton, 2024.

Eliot, T. S. "Little Gidding." In *Four Quartets.* Ecco, 1991.

Hodgman, John. Welcoming Remarks Made at a Literary Reading, September 25, 2001. McSweeneys Internet Tendency. https://tinyurl.com/42dxvjmt.

Kenyon, Jane. "Let Evening Come." In *Collected Poems.* Graywolf, 2005.

Orwell, George. *1984.* Berkeley Reprint, 2003.

Zinsser, William. *On Writing Well.* HarperReference, 1991.